The
Splintered
Market

The Canadian Institute for Economic Policy has been established to engage in public discussion of fiscal, industrial and other related public policies designed to strengthen Canada in a rapidly changing international environment.

The Institute fulfills this mandate by sponsoring and undertaking studies pertaining to the economy of Canada and disseminating such studies. Its intention is to contribute in an innovative way to the development of public policy in Canada.

Canadian Institute for Economic Policy
Suite 409 350 Sparks St., Ottawa K1R 7S8

The Splintered Market

Barriers to Interprovincial Trade in Canadian Agriculture

R.E. Haack, D.R. Hughes and
R.G. Shapiro

Canadian Institute for Economic Policy

The opinions expressed in this study are those of the authors alone and are not intended to represent those of any organization with which they may be associated.

ISBN 0-88862-517-0 cloth
ISBN 0-88862-516-2 paper

6 5 4 3 2 1   81 82 83 84 85 86

Canadian Cataloguing in Publication Data
  Haack, Richard E.
    The Splintered Market

ISBN 0-88862-517-0 (bound).—ISBN 0-88862-516-2 (pbk.)

1. Agriculture—Economic aspects—Canada.
2. Interprovincial commerce—Canada. 3. Agriculture and state—Canada. I. Hughes, D. R. II. Shapiro, R. G. III. Title.

HD1785.H32 1981 338.1′8971   C81-094584-3

Additional copies of this book
may be purchased from:

James Lorimer & Company, Publishers
Egerton Ryerson Memorial Building
35 Britain Street
Toronto M5A 1R7, Ontario

Printed and bound in Canada

Contents

Tables

Foreword

Interprovincial barriers to trade have been increasing in recent years. However, while there is growing evidence of this phenomenon, little systematic research has been undertaken to assess the importance of such barriers in specific sectors.

The Canadian Institute for Economic Policy has sponsored this study to highlight the growing number and complexity of interprovincial barriers to trade in one area vital to the Canadian economy—agriculture. The authors have identified several major areas where interprovincial barriers to trade in food and agriculture exist.

This particular illustration of interprovincial barriers to trade indicates that the challenge to Canadian federal and provincial authorities is to cooperate in the development of regulations that are acceptable to all concerned and that will ensure a stable domestic economic environment.

The Institute hopes that this study will encourage public discussion of this issue. Like all our studies, the views expressed here are those of the authors and do not necessarily reflect those of the Institute.

Roger Voyer
Executive Director
Canadian Institute for Economic Policy

Introduction

Interprovincial barriers to trade in agricultural and food products in Canada is a topical and contentious subject. It is one in which government departments and agencies express an immediate interest and which, indeed, they are in the process of studying themselves. The general perception is that there has been a growth in restraints to trade between the provinces, reflecting such salient features as:

- the policy thrusts of individual provinces—for example, through programs emphasizing provincial self-sufficiency in food products;
- the policy thrusts of the federal government (in concert with provincial authorities) which have, for example, institutionalized market-sharing agreements between the provinces;
- the activities of some provincial and federal marketing boards and agencies that have utilized their market power to restrain trade in competitive products.

The concern about the perceived growth in interprovincial trade barriers is not simply associated with the resultant economic losses and distortions. There is also a fear that a growing acceptance of provincial agricultural balkanization presents a threat to political unity in Canada. Given the level of concern, it is surprising that there is a paucity of empirical research to confirm or deny the perceived growth of interprovincial barriers to trade. This gap in available information is addressed in this study, the major objectives of which are to identify and delineate interprovincial barriers to trade and to discuss, in qualitative terms, their impact on the Canadian food system.

In compiling data for this study, the researchers visited each province and interviewed over two hundred persons. Information sources included the federal Departments of Agriculture, Industry, Trade and Commerce, Consumer and Corporate Affairs, and Regional Economic Expansion, and the relevant provincial ministries in each province. In the private sector, interested trade associations, such as the Retail Council of Canada, Canadian Meat Council, Grocery Products Manufacturers of Canada, Canadian Wine Institute, and Canadian and Ontario Food Processors Associations, were canvassed, as well as federal and provincial marketing boards and other individuals involved in the food system at various levels. Those interviewed were asked to discuss their perceptions of interprovincial barriers to trade with regard to the food or agricultural products that they dealt with. Barriers were defined to include trade distortions created by government intervention in the marketplace, and as a consequence, discussions were wide ranging. For the most part, information was freely given and opinions were expressed candidly.

It bears emphasizing that the material presented here essentially describes how the problem of trade impediments is perceived in the agriculture and food sectors. An effort has been made, however, to sketch in some of the historical background of specific programs and policies, and to review published material that has influenced or reflects thinking on the issues involved.

Clarification of Issues and Objectives

From a legal or constitutional point of view, the concern about impediments to interprovincial trade arises from section 121 of the British North America Act, which states, "All Articles of the Growth, Produce, or Manufacture of any one of the Provinces shall, from and after the Union, be admitted free into each of the other Provinces."

The federal government was given certain powers that in emergency or "greater common good" situations have been used to override the intent of section 121. The provinces, however, have no such powers and their actions are supposedly subject to this clause.

From an economic point of view, the concern about impediments to trade arises from their tendency to reduce the benefits of economic integration. It has been argued that section 121 was meant to guarantee a common market for goods within the Confederation. However, interpretation by the courts has most often resulted in the opinion that the section refers to free movement only in the sense that no tariffs shall apply. (See Appendix A for a more detailed discussion of the constitutional context of the issues dealt with in this study.)

The economic literature dealing with economic integration has emphasized the ways in which nation-states have entered into various forms of economic union. Much of the stimulus for the writing on this subject has been the formation of the European Economic Community, the European Free Trade Association, the Latin American Free Trade

Area, and other experiments in economic integration in the post-war years. The concept is nevertheless extremely relevant to the economic and political union of the British colonies in North America in 1867. Confederation involved a fairly high degree of economic integration among the colonies, and the present Canadian economy is even more highly integrated.

It is perhaps best to establish where Canada fits in the spectrum of economic integration, a spectrum that has been described as follows:

- A free trade area involves only a small degree of integration. Tariffs and quantitative restrictions on trade between members are removed but each member maintains its own barriers against non-members.
- A customs union is similar to a free trade area except that members equalize their tariffs on trade with non-members.
- A common market involves even more integration in that factors of production (labour and capital) are free to move between the member countries.
- Economic union includes all the features of a common market, plus the harmonizing of the national economic policies of the members.
- Total economic integration involves complete unification of monetary, fiscal and social policies.

The Canadian economy is integrated more fully than that described as a common market or even an economic union, since a single monetary system exists and monetary policy is implemented by the federal government. Yet Canada is not totally integrated economically, since the provinces have independent roles in several aspects of fiscal and social policy.

The reasons for seeking economic integration are numerous and will not be dealt with at length here. Generally, increased integration of markets will provide net economic gains to the economy as a whole. Integration means larger markets, which in turn mean a greater division of labour and the attendant economic benefits.

The production of goods and services tends to shift to regions where it is comparatively most efficient. Mobile factors of production tend to shift to locations where they are most productive. Competition increases, creating pressure for improvement in methods of production and a reduction of local monopoly. The result is an increased level of income for the community as a whole.

An emphasis on free movement of goods detracts somewhat from the more general issue of economic integration. Presumably, the members of the Canadian confederation desire the benefits associated with a highly integrated national economy and are interested in maintaining or increasing those benefits by ensuring the free movement of products (goods and services) and factors of production (labour and capital) between provinces. The objective of this study, then, is to examine the nature and extent of forces that reduce the degree of economic integration in agricultural markets. Important aspects of this particular issue are the extents to which the free movement between provinces of agricultural products and the factors used in agricultural production has been, or is being, impeded.

It must be kept in mind, however, that the achievement of a high degree of economic integration and its attendant benefits was not the sole purpose of Confederation, nor is it the sole objective of economic and social policy in Canada today. Other social, cultural and political objectives are also important. In some cases these other objectives are pursued through methods that reduce the degree of integration in the economy.

The federal form of government itself creates some impediments to the achievement of a truly integrated economy. For instance, complete integration implies uniform policies for all members of the community. Any variation with regard to taxes, expenditures or regulations among regions would automatically give some regions artificial advantages or disadvantages with respect to other regions. And yet the essence of federal government is the division of powers between federal and provincial jurisdictions. Some variation in taxes, public expenditures, and the regulatory environment will inevitably exist among provinces in policy areas that are a provincial responsibility. A.E. Safarian has succinctly summarized the problem in his discussion of agricultural marketing legislation:

> It bears emphasis that there is a larger issue here which has to be faced squarely in any scheme, whether federal or federal-provincial. There is a distinction between regulation (as distinct from a free market solution) whose purpose is to achieve an efficient allocation of resources and regulation whose purpose is to reinforce a purely provincial market. For products which are easily transportable, the latter amounts to a denial of a common market for goods, whether it is achieved by federal regulation alone, by federal-provincial regulation, or by the federal government permitting or empowering others to regulate. Whatever the other objectives of regulation, one should keep clearly in mind the need for an efficient allocation of production within the common market, rather than simply within provincial boundaries.[1]

---

[1] A.E. Safarian, *Canadian Federalism and Economic Integration* (Ottawa: Information Canada, 1974), p. 56.

The relevant question, then, is whether the actions of federal and provincial governments are consistent with the maintenance of a high degree of economic integration. Where they are not, the importance of the objectives being pursued in relation to the economic benefits being foregone must be carefully weighed.

Transportation 1

As a result of the large distances between markets across Canada, transportation issues play a major role in the interprovincial movement of food and agricultural products. Three aspects of transportation-related interprovincial barriers are addressed here: direct and indirect regional freight subsidies, provincial truck licencing regulations, and transport equipment availability.

Freight Subsidies

The federal government provides direct and indirect subsidies for the movement of specified products. The history of these programs is long and complex, reflecting an early recognition that freight rates can have a profound effect on resource allocation in the economy. For example, between 1917 and 1920 cumulative railroad rate increases in Central Canada totalled 111 per cent, while in the Maritimes increases ranged between 140 and 216 per cent. These sharp upward adjustments were caused by wartime inflation as well as a "levelling-up" of rates to effect rate-equalization across Canada. Producers in the Maritimes found that their ability to compete in the rest of Canada was adversely affected by the new rate structure. The total number of persons employed in manufacturing in the region from 1919 to 1921 declined by nearly 42 per cent. Of course, rate changes were only one factor contributing to this regional decline, albeit a major one. The post-war Depression and a shift from coal to hydroelectric and petroleum energy sources were other important influences.

The major transportation subsidy programs administered by the federal government are the Maritime and Atlantic freight subsidies, the Crow's Nest Pass rates, and Feed Freight Assistance. Within the ambit of this study, only a brief historical-political overview of each of these programs and a review of their respective salient provisions are presented.

Maritime Freight Rates Act

The Maritime Freight Rates Act (MFRA), which became effective on 1 July 1927, is the founding legislation for transportation subsidies in the Atlantic region. The Royal Commission on Maritime Claims (Duncan Commission) found that Maritime rail rates had risen more rapidly than elsewhere in Canada during the 1912–25 period, and in conformity with federal promises of competitive access to Central Canada for Maritime products, the commission recommended the subsidy program. The act required the Canadian National Railways to reduce certain rates by 20 per cent within the three Maritime provinces and that part of Quebec situated east of Levis and Diamond, and south of the St. Lawrence River. In 1949 the island of Newfoundland was included. The MFRA further required the railways to reduce their rates on traffic moving outbound from the Atlantic region to other parts of Canada by 20 per cent. The reductions applied only to the Atlantic portion of the haul.

In 1975 the subsidy on rail traffic from the Atlantic region to other parts of Canada was increased from 20 per cent to 30 per cent (that is, a 30 per cent reduction on the Atlantic region portion of the rate) to offset a greater incidence of competitive rate "hold downs" outside the Atlantic region and "horizontal" rate increases across Canada, which resulted in a higher increase in absolute terms for long-haul shippers.

The reductions under the MFRA did not apply to the following traffic movements: traffic to or from the United States; eastbound traffic originating west of Levis and Diamond; import traffic from overseas; export traffic via ports west of Levis and Diamond; passenger and express[1] movements.

Atlantic Region Freight Assistance Act

On 15 July 1969 the Atlantic Region Freight Assistance Act (ARFAA) provided for-hire truckers with approximately the same level of assistance as the railways on traffic from the Atlantic region. A year later truck traffic moving between points in this region and rail express traffic moving westbound from the region were accorded a 17.5 per cent subsidy.

Since 1970 there have been numerous subsidy rate changes for both

---

[1] Express moving outbound from the Atlantic region to other parts of Canada became eligible for the MFRA subsidy in 1969 under the Atlantic Region Freight Assistance Act, while express movements within the Atlantic region became eligible in 1975 under Orders of the Canadian Transport Commission.

rail and truck movement of goods, as well as selective commodity coverage for both westbound and intraregional movements. The Atlantic Region Selective Assistance Regulations, effective 15 April 1974, provided for a subsidy of 20 per cent over and above the 30 per cent westbound subsidy to cover the movement of a selected list of eligible commodities from points in the Atlantic region to other parts of Canada. This additional subsidy is payable to both railways and for-hire truckers in return for reducing their rates by amounts authorized by the Canadian Transport Commission. Eligible commodities include unprocessed agricultural and fisheries products, along with commodities manufactured in the region for which the full potential for adding value is achieved within the region. Marine and air modes of transport are also now subsidized on a selective commodity basis.

Table 1-1 shows the subsidies payable to eligible carriers under the MFRA and ARFAA on movements outbound from the Atlantic region. Although the Canadian Transport Commission records the trade flow whenever a subsidy is paid, summary data on product movements are not available. The Quebec government has charged that the Maritime subsidies adversely affect the Gaspé region of that province. However, a current unpublished study has brought into question the validity of this complaint by demonstrating that subsidies on movement out of the Gaspé exceed those on movement out of the Atlantic provinces.[2]

Crow's Nest Pass Statutory Rates
The "Crow" rate originated with an agreement between the federal government and the Canadian Pacific Railway in 1897. Canadian Pacific was anxious to build a railway line from Lethbridge through the Crow's Nest Pass to Nelson, British Columbia, in order to obtain access to attractive coal and mineral deposits in that region. Since sufficient funding for this project was not available from private sources, Canadian Pacific and the Government of Canada entered into an agreement by which the government subsidized the construction of the Crow's Nest line in return for the railway's promise to transport grain out of the Prairie region at a reduced rate. Reduced rates on agricultural implements, building materials, and other products moving from Eastern Canada into the Prairie region were also agreed upon. Canadian Pacific was able to build the desired line, and the government had acquired a concession that would be of substantial help in efforts to develop agriculture on the Prairies. The rates agreed to in 1897 were

---

[2] Background information with regard to the MFRA and ARFAA was obtained from discussions with Transport Canada and Agriculture Canada personnel.

TABLE 1-1

EXAMPLES OF THE SUBSIDIES PAYABLE TO ELIGIBLE CARRIERS UNDER THE MARITIME FREIGHT RATES ACT AND ATLANTIC REGION FREIGHT ASSISTANCE ACT ON MOVEMENTS OUTBOUND FROM THE ATLANTIC REGION

(all figures are percentages)

COL. A: Basic 30%* subsidy that is already reflected as a reduction in the carriers' published rates to the extent required.

COL. B: Additional 20%* subsidy on "selective" commodities that applies as a reduction from the carriers' published rates.

COL. C: Total subsidy.

												To
From	Montreal, Que.			Toronto, Ont.			Winnipeg, Man.			Vancouver, B.C.		
	A	B	C	A	B	C	A	B	C	A	B	C
St. John's, Nfld.	26.4	17.6	44.0	22.3	14.9	37.2	15.3	10.2	25.5	9.9	6.6	16.5
Corner Brook, Nfld.	25.5	16.8	42.0	20.3	13.6	33.9	12.9	8.6	21.5	7.9	5.3	13.2
Yarmouth, N.S.	24.6	16.4	41.0	19.3	12.9	32.2	11.7	7.8	19.5	7.0	4.7	11.7
Sydney, N.S.	24.0	16.0	40.0	18.5	12.3	30.8	10.9	7.3	18.2	6.4	4.3	10.7
Halifax, N.S.	22.9	15.3	38.2	17.0	11.3	28.3	9.5	6.3	15.8	5.4	3.6	9.0
Charlottetown, P.E.I.	22.5	15.0	37.5	16.4	10.9	27.3	9.0	6.0	15.0	5.1	3.4	8.5
Moncton, N.B.	20.8	13.9	34.7	14.2	9.5	23.7	7.3	4.9	12.2	4.0	2.7	6.7
Edmundston, N.B.	15.0	10.0	25.0	8.6	5.7	14.3	3.8	2.5	6.3	1.9	1.3	3.2

*Based on the proportion that the haul within the Atlantic region is to the total haul.

Source: Unpublished information supplied by Transport Canada.

revised upward several times in the ensuing years but remained at levels well below rates applied to transportation of similar commodities. By the mid-1920s the rates had reached levels about 25 per cent above their original level. Elimination of the statutory rates was seriously considered in the mid-1920s, but the interests of Prairie grain producers prevailed in Parliament. The rates were not eliminated; instead they were reduced to the original levels negotiated in 1897 and have remained unchanged since.

Originally the rate reductions were to apply to: "grain and flour from all points . . . west of Fort William to Port Arthur and points east." The objective of these reductions was clearly to reduce the cost of moving Prairie grains into an export position. This overall objective was maintained over the years as the grain-handling system changed or as new crops were introduced. For instance, West Coast ports (Vancouver and Prince Rupert) and Churchill were subsequently included among the destinations to which the statutory rates applied. With the opening of the St. Lawrence Seaway, policies relevant to transportation east of Thunder Bay changed. The development of rapeseed as a major crop led to the addition of this crop to the list of eligible "grain." Of the products of rapeseed crushing (meal and oil), only rapeseed meal became eligible for transportation at the statutory rate. (Examples of the statutory rates that prevailed in 1977, substantially the same as those negotiated in 1897, are presented in Table 1-2.)

It is not surprising that the railways became reluctant to transport grain at these rates as time passed. Manifestations of this were the continuing pressure on the part of the railways to be allowed to discontinue service on some branch lines, and a reluctance to replace rolling stock used in grain transportation. As a result, the federal government has become involved in the subsidization of maintenance costs on "grain dependent" branch lines.

Expenditures have also been made by the federal government to rehabilitate boxcars the railways would otherwise have removed from service and for the purchase of new hopper cars. The Canadian Wheat Board and the governments of the three Prairie provinces have also become involved in the purchase and/or leasing of hopper cars to maintain adequate rolling stock for grain transportation.

The grain-handling system and the Crow rates have been the subject of several commissions and considerable formal and informal evaluation and discussion throughout this century, but especially in the last twenty years. In 1976 the Commission on the Costs of Transporting Grain by Rail (commonly known as the Snavely Commission) produced an estimate of the costs and revenues involved in the transportation of grain at statutory rates.

TABLE 1-2
STATUTORY RAIL FREIGHT RATES, 1977
(¢'s per 100 lbs.)

	Rate to		
		Vancouver and	
	Thunder Bay	*Prince Rupert*	*Churchill*
Commodity and shipping point	Domestic and export	Export only	
Grain and grain products			
Dawson Creek, B.C.	38	25	36
Calgary, Alta.	26	20	26
Edmonton, Alta.	26	20	25
Regina, Sask.	20	26	22
Saskatoon, Sask.	22	24	21
Winnipeg, Man.	14	34	23

Flaxseed and rapeseed:
All rates 1.5 cents per 100 pounds higher than the grain and grain products rates for the same distance—e.g., Calgary to Thunder Bay: 27.5 cents per 100 pounds.

Source: CPR, CNR and BCR tariffs as reported by Peter Arcus in "The Impact of Changes in the Statutory Freight Rates for Grain," *Freight Rates and the Marketing of Canadian Agricultural Products* (Winnipeg: Department of Agricultural Economics and Farm Management, University of Manitoba, August 1977).

Table 1-3 presents an analysis of how the costs of transportation of statutory grain by rail were covered. Users of the service paid 21.8 cents per hundredweight, which represented 38.3 per cent of the total cost of grain transportation as estimated by the commission. This amount represents payments for transportation at Crow rates and corresponds to the sample rates presented in Table 1-2. The remaining 62.7 per cent (35.15 cents per hundredweight) of the total cost of transporting grain at statutory rates was made up of a 23.6 per cent subsidy by the federal government and a 38.1 per cent subsidy by other users of the rail transportation system.

In the discussions with industry and government officials, upon which this study is based, the Crow rates were most often identified with two closely associated problems. The first is related to the "export subsidy" effect of the statutory rates. It was felt that the rates encourage grain production in the Prairie region and cause less grain to be produced in other parts of Canada than would otherwise be the case. At the same time, transportation of processed products is not subsidized. The rate differential between raw and processed products discourages processing of raw agricultural products within the Prairie region. Virtually everyone commenting on the rate issue admitted that the livestock and food-processing sectors in Western Canada suffer. At the same time, the benefits accruing to grain producers were considered substantial. However, opinions as to the *net* effect on the Prairie economy of increasing grain transportation rates to compensatory levels were widely divergent. Not surprisingly, those that benefit most from the Crow rate (grain producers in Saskatchewan) are the most outspoken defenders of the status quo, whereas those that feel the most disadvantaged (Prairie livestock producers and oilseed crushers) are the strongest proponents of compensatory rates.

TABLE 1-3
COVERAGE OF THE TOTAL COSTS INCURRED IN 1974 FOR
THE TRANSPORTATION OF STATUTORY GRAIN BY RAIL

Source of cost coverage	*Amount of cost coverage*			*Percentage distribution of coverage*
	Total $'s (millions)	*$'s per ton*	*¢'s per 100 lbs.*	
Users of the service	89.7	4.36	21.80	38.3
Federal government	55.4	2.69	13.45	23.6
Railways	89.3	4.34	21.70	38.1
Total	234.4	11.39	56.95	100.0

Source: Office of the Privy Council, *Commission on the Costs of Transporting Grain by Rail: Report*, vol. 1 (Ottawa: Department of Supply and Services, October 1976).

The second problem is related to the transportation subsidy on feed grain for domestic consumption, which the Crow rate represents. In this case feed grains shipped out of the Prairie region for consumption in Eastern Canada move as far as Thunder Bay at statutory rates. The reduction of transportation costs then becomes an important element of feed grain policy in Canada, which also involves Feed Freight Assistance and certain aspects of the Canadian Wheat Board's operations.

Past and present policies with respect to feed grains for domestic consumption were identified as major impediments to trade.

Feed Freight Assistance

The name Feed Freight Assistance has become associated with the program under which transportation of feed grains from the Prairie region to Eastern Canada and British Columbia is subsidized. These subsidies were initially provided for under the War Measures Act. The first payments to shippers were made in 1941, and although the policy has undergone some substantial alterations, it has remained in effect to the present time. The rationale for the implementation of this policy was closely related to circumstances prevailing in Canadian agriculture immediately prior to and during the first years of the Second World War. A lack of demand for wheat revealed itself in extremely rapid increases in inventories—from 24 million bushels in 1938 to 595 million bushels in 1943. At the same time there was a rapid increase in the demand for livestock products as a result of the war in Europe.

To deal with the situation, several programs were initiated by the government. Delivery quotas on wheat were implemented, and incentives to reduce wheat acreage were provided through the Wheat Acreage Reduction Act (1941). At the same time, increased production of feed grains was encouraged through direct subsidies, and fertilizer and lime subsidies. Subsidized transportation of feed grains and assistance in the processing of livestock feeds were also implemented to encourage livestock production.

Many of these programs lapsed as circumstances changed, but the transportation subsidy has remained in effect up to the present time. Feed Freight Assistance was undoubtedly an important factor in the rapid increase in livestock production in Central and Eastern Canada during the war years.

In 1948 the Canadian Wheat Board was made the sole selling agency for barley and oats, giving the board a control over these grains similar to that which it was already exercising with respect to wheat. As a result, the Wheat Board could, and did, price Prairie feed grains in Eastern Canada and British Columbia in such a way that Feed Freight Assistance subsidies were effectively captured by Prairie grain producers.

Over the years situations arose in which feed grain prices prevailing in the Prairie provinces were much lower than those prevailing in Eastern Canada and British Columbia. Depressed feed grain prices in the Prairie provinces were the result of the Canadian Wheat Board's marketing strategy in the domestic market. The board priced feed grains in such a way as to obtain the highest possible price without triggering imports of corn from the United States. Feed grains that the board could not market in Eastern Canada because of lack of demand at "corn competitive prices" remained in storage on Prairie farms. Because the board cannot control intraprovincial grain marketing, this build-up of inventories caused exceptionally low prices to prevail in some or all of the intraprovincial feed grain markets in the provinces of Alberta, Saskatchewan and Manitoba. The situation became particularly acute during the period of slow export sales and rapidly increasing grain inventories that prevailed in the late 1960s. In addition, purchasers of feed grains felt that the board disregarded other considerations important to buyers, such as consistency of supply.

The Canadian Livestock Feed Board was created to provide a "countervailing power" to the Canadian Wheat Board in order to ensure adequate and consistent supplies of feed grains to buyers outside of the Prairie region. In 1974 the new National Feed Grains Policy was introduced. Several significant changes were made in policies to create a "free" domestic market for feed grains. The power to price, and to control the movement of, feed grains for domestic consumption was removed from the Canadian Wheat Board. Users of feed grain throughout Canada had direct access to western grain. Sellers, including farmers, were allowed to sell feed grain on the domestic market throughout Canada.

Several modifications to the National Feed Grains Policy were made in subsequent years. Due to strong export demand, domestic feed grain prices prevailing after the implementation of the new policy were generally above corn competitive prices in Eastern Canada. In 1976 the Wheat Board agreed to offer feed grains at corn competitive prices. This was apparently implemented to ensure the use of Canadian grains by buyers in Eastern Canada, rather than of corn imported from the U.S.A. This has led to the complaint by Prairie grain producers that the policy no longer represents a free market, but one in which a ceiling price prevails.[3] At the same time that corn competitive pricing was announced, the elimination or reduction of subsidies under Feed Freight Assistance was put into effect. Subsidies remained unchanged on movement of feed grains into northern and eastern Quebec and the Atlantic provinces. Subsidies were reduced on movement into British Columbia, some parts of northeastern Ontario and central Quebec. Subsidies were eliminated on movement into most parts of Ontario and

---

[3] Saskatchewan Natural Products Marketing Council, "The Domestic Feed Grain Market Performance: 1976 to 1979," pamphlet.

a small region in the western part of Quebec. Funds freed due to reduced subsidy payments were directed toward improving grain storage facilities in the affected regions. The impact of movement of domestic feed grains on the grain-handling system in Western Canada became a concern in the years following the introduction of the new policy. To ensure that domestic feed grains would not unduly disrupt the grain-handling system, the Wheat Board instituted quota and other controls on domestic feed grains entering the grain-handling system.

The relative importance of Feed Freight Assistance in comparison with some other federal programs is shown in Table 1-4. Expenditures under the Canadian Livestock Feed Board (of which Feed Freight Assistance is a major part) are roughly comparable to expenditures under the Maritime and Atlantic freight subsidy schemes. While these expenditures are not the largest that the federal government undertakes, they are nevertheless substantial. The regional distribution of shipments under Feed Freight Assistance is shown in Table 1-5. Noteworthy are the importance of Quebec, which accounts for approximately half of the shipments, and the rapid decline in shipments into Ontario due to increasing corn production and the virtual elimination of Feed Freight Assistance in that province.

It is evident from the cursory examination of the Feed Freight Assistance policy that its effects have been intricately linked to related policy areas such as the Canadian Wheat Board, the Canadian Livestock Feed Board and the National Feed Grains Policy. During the Second World War the policy proved effective in increasing livestock production in Eastern Canada. Due to the Wheat Board's ability to set prices in the post-war period, Feed Freight Assistance became a subsidy to Prairie grain producers.[4] With the advent of the National Feed Grains Policy, Feed Freight Assistance is having the effect that would normally be expected from such a subsidy; that is, it favours the production of feed grains in the Prairies over production in Eastern Canada and British Columbia, and it favours livestock production in Eastern Canada and British Columbia over production in the Prairies.

Almost everyone interviewed in the Prairie provinces mentioned Feed Freight Assistance as an important impediment to interprovincial trade because of the artificial advantage it gives to livestock feeders outside of the Prairie region. Corn competitive pricing of barley by the Wheat Board is also causing concern—especially in 1980 when barley supplies in the Prairies were short. In the words of one interviewee,

---

[4] T.C. Kerr, *An Economic Analysis of the Feed Freight Assistance Policy* (Ottawa: Agricultural Economics Research Council of Canada, 1966).

TABLE 1-4
NET EXPENDITURES BY FEDERAL GOVERNMENT FOR SELECTED POLICIES AND PROGRAMS
(thousands of $'s)

	1970/71	1971/72	1972/73	1973/74	1974/75	1975/76	1976/77	1977/78	1978/79
Canadian Livestock Feed Board (Feed Freight Assistance)	20,773	20,653	21,381	22,737	21,921	20,709	12,730	11,773	14,155
Purchase of grain hopper cars	—	—	46,091	—	—	40,639	167,341	2,343	838
Maritime Freight Rates Act	13,999	13,111	13,000	14,088	15,060	16,020	17,103	15,986	15,379
Atlantic Region Freight Assistance	2,822	6,937	11,422	15,972	21,748	23,692	27,070	29,907	41,283
Direct milk subsidy	125,000	109,000	107,400	143,400	251,100	275,000	233,118	293,580	271,524
Crop insurance	3,818	4,035	5,214	16,655	31,236	48,276	56,457	72,812	74,965
Research	59,128	64,257	69,663	81,151	98,132	130,033	133,219	143,654	152,276

Sources: Agriculture Canada, *Orientation of Canadian Agriculture* (Ottawa: 1977); Receiver General for Canada, *Public Accounts of Canada.*

11

TABLE 1-5
FREIGHT ASSISTED SHIPMENTS OF FEEDS BY PROVINCE OF DESTINATION
(thousand tonnes)

Province	1968/69	1969/70	1970/71	1971/72	1972/73	1973/74	1974/75	1975/76	1976/77	1977/78	1978/79
Newfoundland	34.6	31.9	36.6	39.0	33.8	34.6	34.4	28.4	45.4	34.5	42.5
Prince Edward Island	27.9	25.9	41.2	42.0	35.7	39.1	25.2	26.0	15.6	28.9	38.5
Nova Scotia	146.6	156.0	162.7	174.4	177.8	170.6	179.0	170.3	164.4	176.2	205.4
New Brunswick	92.6	95.8	96.7	97.9	100.4	97.2	98.1	93.1	94.3	110.3	114.4
Quebec	1,019.3	1,173.8	1,299.6	1,275.1	1,437.5	1,286.0	1,314.0	1,159.6	1,040.0	1,111.4	1,445.1
Ontario	561.3	935.9	726.3	553.9	690.7	675.8	639.2	462.9	78.1	12.6	15.2
British Columbia	285.1	308.2	338.6	325.0	331.9	321.1	287.7	266.3	255.7	307.8	426.3
Total	2,167.4	2,727.5	2,701.7	2,507.3	2,807.8	2,624.4	2,577.6	2,206.6	1,693.5	1,781.7	2,287.5

Sources: Canada Grains Council, *Canadian Grains Industry Statistical Handbook 1979*, Winnipeg: Canadian Livestock Feed Board, *Annual Reports*.

"The National Feed Grains Policy insures adequate supplies of Western feed grains at a corn-competitive price ceiling to all livestock producers in Canada *except* those in the Prairie provinces."

Truck Licencing Regulations

Truck licencing is a matter of provincial jurisdiction, and each province has public commercial vehicle (PCV) licence requirements for truckers using provincial roads, whether the goods originate, terminate or merely pass in-transit through the province. The federal Motor Vehicle Transport Act provides statutory authority for the provincial licencing of interprovincial and in-transit trucking, and each province typically has a Public Commercial Vehicles Act, which regulates the industry. As well, Reciprocity Licencing Agreements between individual provinces supplement the act.

Across Canada, truck licencing required for interprovincial movement of agricultural products is considered a major barrier. This study does not attempt a comprehensive analysis of licencing issues in the trucking industry, but the following examples from interviews indicate the range of problems encountered.

Quebec and Ontario have a reciprocity agreement that provides for the interprovincial movement of "natural farm products" without the requirement of a licence (of course, only PCV's must be licenced for interprovincial trade—a farmer may drive his own product in his own truck without a PCV licence). According to officials at the Ministère du Québec de l'Agriculture, des Pêcheries et de l'Alimentation, the Ontario Department of Transportation and Communications defines this term more narrowly than does Quebec. The produce must be in its first movement from the farm—once it has been graded, washed, packed or processed away from the farm, it is no longer in its first movement and a licence is required.

To obtain such a licence, the applicant must appear before the Ontario Highway Transport Board and convince the board that the issuance of a licence is of public necessity and convenience. The time and costs involved may amount to several years and several thousands of dollars. The Quebec ministry official argued that since the purchasers in Ontario do not wish to buy their produce in the "natural state" as defined, the produce hauler must obtain the licence. Further, it was the impression of the Quebec official (not shared by the Ontario ministry) that the PCV licence for Quebec was relatively inexpensive and could be obtained quickly. The controversy reflects mutual antagonism and indicates a real barrier to the free movement of agricultural products interprovincially.

Produce haulage problems have been experienced in provinces other than Ontario and Quebec as well. Several years ago the British Columbia lettuce growers, attempting to sell their produce in Alberta and the Prairies, were being forced by truck-licencing authorities to use common carriers not adaptable to the type of haulage required for fresh produce (that is, such carriers move only from depot to depot). For many years the licencing authorities would not acknowledge the need for a specialized service, but this matter was resolved in 1979, according to information provided by the lettuce producers' cooperative.

Provincial truck-licencing regulations have created an interprovincial barrier to the movement of all goods in the past. However, very recent developments may reduce truck-licencing impediments to the movement of food and agricultural products between the provinces. In October, a new reciprocity agreement was signed by nine provincial transportation ministers at the Roads and Transportation Association of Canada annual conference in Toronto.

Under the agreement, to be effective in six provinces by April 1981 and in Quebec, Nova Scotia and Newfoundland by April 1982, truck owners will licence their vehicles in their home provinces, paying a prorated portion of the full applicable provincial licence fee according to estimates of mileage to be travelled in that province. The home province transport department will inform the truck owner what percentage will be owed to the other provinces in which he expects to operate. The trucker will then apply by mail for cab cards from the other provinces, each card costing a prorated portion of that province's applicable fee. A trucker entering a province without the appropriate cab card will have to pay the full licence fee for that province for that year. Prince Edward Island, the Yukon and the Northwest Territories abstained from signing the agreement but voiced their approval in principle.[5]

Finally, there is some concern across the provinces that trade unions are limiting the number of stops that an out-of-province trucker can make in a province; however, there was no consensus on this issue.

Availability of Transportation Equipment

An Agriculture Canada source indicated that freight rates from the Maritimes were not so much a barrier to shipment westward as were the lack of "reefer" cars and insulated equipment to handle peak-season produce volumes. He stated that 95 per cent of the railway cars moving carcass beef from Alberta to Montreal return empty to the

---

[5] Reported in the *Globe and Mail*, 3 October 1980.

West, since it is too expensive to shuttle them to the Maritimes. Truck transport is not feasible in P.E.I., since there is a government restriction on truck sizes because of poor-quality roads, and potato producers have, as yet, been unable to organize to build a central storage area accessible to trucks.

Another very visible example of equipment shortages can be seen in the grain transportation problems currently being faced in Western Canada. The railways became increasingly reluctant to replace rolling stock, as haulage of grain became less and less desirable because of rising costs and the fixed returns associated with statutory rates. To maintain adequate capacity, various governments have been forced to buy and/or lease rolling stock, since the railways have refused to do so. Difficulty in obtaining grain transportation services is seen, in both Eastern and Western Canada, as an impediment to interprovincial trade.

The general point to be made is that inadequate transportation facilities can constrain movement of agricultural and other products. The pertinent question, therefore, is: Why are some transportation facilities inadequate? In part, this inadequacy reflects the impact of regulations on transportation. For example, controlled rates, or less than compensatory subsidy programs, can predispose the transportation companies not to reinvest in needed capital stock. The reluctance of the railway companies to invest in railway stock to transport Prairie grain and Maritime potatoes are two cases in point.

Marketing Boards   2

Marketing board activities are frequently associated with the restriction of interprovincial trade. In the discussions with government officials, academics and people in the private sector across Canada, three major areas of concern were apparent. The most important concern related to the rigidity of production patterns associated with the market-sharing feature of the national supply management marketing boards (industrial milk, eggs, chickens and turkeys). Another important concern relates to the effect of the regulatory powers of marketing boards upon interprovincial movement of products. Specifically, pricing and licencing powers were identified as actual or potential barriers to the free movement of products. Finally, many marketing boards control where and how producers market their products. Most often this means that producers must deliver to a provincial agency, thus precluding delivery outside of the province. This outright restriction of interprovincial movement at the producer level may or may not have a serious impact on trade flows. For example, while individual producers are not free to deliver hogs in other provinces, pork products move freely between provinces with the result that little distortion in hog and pork markets takes place. In contrast, restrictions on the interprovincial movement of Prairie grains were associated with significant distortions in the Canadian feed grains market prior to 1974.[1]

It is important to clearly relate such problems to the particular marketing boards involved. The historical development of marketing boards is also important because it has been strongly influenced by problems related to interprovincial and international trade.

Development and Evolution of Marketing Boards

The first marketing boards in Canada were essentially compulsory cooperatives. An early attempt to make an already existing voluntary

---

[1] T.C. Kerr, *An Economic Analysis of the Feed Freight Assistance Policy* (Ottawa: Agricultural Economics Research Council of Canada, 1966), pp. 55-56.

cooperative into a marketing board involved a cooperative formed by Okanagan tree fruit growers in 1913. The cooperative operated with mixed success for several years. The problems encountered arose from the cooperative's lack of market power. Cooperatives have only very limited control over the marketing activities of members, and no control over those of non-members. With a view to creating an organization with compulsory membership, the legislature of British Columbia passed the Produce Marketing Act in 1927. The act established a "Committee of Direction," which was given power to regulate all aspects of the marketing of tree fruits, including pricing, collection of a levy, and administration of an equalization fund. This act was declared *ultra vires* in 1931 on the grounds that it regulated interprovincial trade and that the levy constituted an indirect tax, both of which are beyond the legislative authority of a province.

Failure to obtain appropriate legislation at the provincial level led to pressure for federal legislation of a similar nature. The Natural Products Marketing Act was passed in 1934. Under the act, the federal government could either exercise marketing powers directly or delegate them to local producers' boards. This federal act was also declared *ultra vires* because the federal government could not regulate trade of a local nature—that is to say, within a province. Since neither level of government could provide boards with control over both intra- and interprovincial aspects of marketing, subsequent developments involved provincial legislation that allowed boards to regulate the intraprovincial aspects only. Although this limited the effectiveness of some boards, the number of boards increased steadily. It was even possible to establish effective supply management programs within the framework of provincial regulation for difficult-to-transport commodities such as fluid milk.

The powers of provincial boards were augmented considerably through the federal Agricultural Products Marketing Act of 1949. An important feature of the act was the implementation of a method by which boards could exercise control over both intra- and interprovincial trade. Essentially, the problem of split jurisdictions between the provincial and federal legislatures was circumvented by having each jurisdiction delegate the appropriate powers to a third party, that is, the marketing board. In this way the marketing board could exercise control over the intraprovincial aspects of its activities through powers delegated from the provincial government, and over the interprovincial and export aspects of its activities through powers delegated from the federal government.

The system of provincial boards worked adequately for many years. Early in the 1970s, however, a situation developed in which marketing boards for chickens and for eggs in some provinces took a competitive rather than a cooperative approach toward each other. The result was a trade war (the "chicken and egg war"). To overcome these difficulties, the Farm Products Marketing Agencies Act was passed and implemented in 1972. The important feature of the "national" agencies created under the Farm Products Marketing Agencies Act is an explicit agreement between the various provincial marketing boards to share the national market in a specified manner, thus eliminating the possibility of further trade wars. The presence of such a national supply management scheme also allows the federal government to institute import controls on the subject commodities, thus protecting the national boards from international competition.[2]

It is evident from this cursory examination of the evolution of marketing boards that, at least for some boards, problems related to interprovincial trade in their commodities have been a major cause of innovation in board powers and structures. While none of the boards have the objective of preventing interprovincial trade, many of the powers delegated to boards are aimed at enabling them to control interprovincial trade in such a way as to prevent undesirable situations such as trade wars.

National Supply Management Marketing Boards

At the present time there are three marketing boards operating under the Farm Products Marketing Agencies Act: the Canadian Egg Marketing Agency (CEMA), the Canadian Chicken Marketing Agency (CCMA) and the Canadian Turkey Marketing Agency (CTMA). In addition, the regulation of the industrial milk market by the Canadian Dairy Commission involves the operation of a national supply management scheme similar to those operated by CEMA, CCMA and CTMA.

The Canadian Dairy Commission

The Canadian Dairy Commission (CDC) is a Crown corporation created by the Canadian Dairy Commission Act, 1966. The commission's activities include price support through offers to purchase butter, skim milk powder and cheese; storage and export programs to dispose of excess supplies acquired through the offer-to-purchase programs; administration of subsidies; product promotion; collection of levies and quota allocation. The commission is concerned only with the regulation

---

[2] As a member of the General Agreement on Tariffs and Trade, Canada is committed not to implement import quotas for commodities that are not subject to regulation of supplies at the national level.

of industrial milk,[3] but works closely with provincial milk marketing boards. The provincial boards' primary responsibility is the regulation of fluid milk markets,[4] but they also carry out many of the administrative aspects of the industrial milk policy.

In the course of the research for this study, two concerns were voiced about the operations of the Canadian Dairy Commission with regard to impediments to interprovincial trade. The first concern, which applies to all national supply management boards, was that the system of quota allocation between provinces introduced rigidity into production patterns. The original allocation of the national industrial milk market between provinces and in several subsequent years is given in Table 2-1. It is possible, of course, that no relocation of production activity would have taken place even in the absence of a market-sharing agreement among the provinces. On the other hand, the present system impedes the relocation of production where it is called for by changes in population distribution, by technological change favouring production in a particular region, or by other circumstances that alter comparative advantage between regions.

The second concern had to do with the butter-pricing policy of the

TABLE 2-1
ORIGINAL AND SUBSEQUENT PROVINCIAL SHARES OF THE NATIONAL INDUSTRIAL MILK MARKET
(%)

Province	Original allocation	1 April 1976	1 April 1978	1 August 1979
P.E.I.	1.58	1.39	1.87	1.88
Nova Scotia	.93	1.17	1.21	1.21
New Brunswick	1.02	1.28	1.32	1.33
Quebec	44.42	48.11	47.96	47.96
Ontario	33.59	31.67	31.31	31.32
Manitoba	4.42	3.95	3.91	3.90
Saskatchewan	3.32	2.50	2.59	2.60
Alberta	8.13	6.80	6.70	6.71
British Columbia	2.60	3.13	3.09	3.09

Source: Canadian Dairy Commission, *Annual Report* (Ottawa), various issues.

---

[3] "Industrial milk" is used in the manufacture of dairy products such as butter, cheese, skim milk powder, yogurt, ice cream, et cetera.

[4] "Fluid milk" is used for consumption as fresh milk and cream.

CDC. The commission's purchase and selling prices are the same in all parts of Canada. Some industry participants, in Western Canada particularly, felt that this deprived them of the higher prices that would normally prevail if prices in Western Canada were allowed to reflect the cost of transportation from Eastern Canada. It was felt that this discriminated against industrial milk producers in the West. In fact, this policy was cited as one reason that British Columbia producers evidence little interest in filling their industrial milk quota.

The Canadian Egg Marketing Agency

The Canadian Egg Marketing Agency establishes a "global" production quota based on anticipated market demand for table eggs. The global, or national, quota is allocated between provinces according to predetermined shares. The initial market shares were based on production during the five-year period from 1967 to 1971 and have remained unchanged (see Table 2-2). Prices in each province are developed from a national average price for grade "A" eggs (basis Toronto) and from specific assumptions about transportation costs and traditional trade flows (surplus/deficit regions). Eggs surplus to consumer demand for table use are purchased by CEMA and resold to egg processors (breakers) for industrial purposes. Care was taken in the formulation of the federal-provincial agreement, which underlies the agency's formation, to ensure that prices would be set with due regard to: 1) a cost of production formula; and 2) free interprovincial trade. However, the national quota allocation between provinces is based on negotiable but nevertheless rigid market shares. An Alberta retailer claimed that he is forced to import 60 per cent of his total egg requirements from Manitoba and Saskatchewan because Alberta's market share has not increased in proportion to population and economic activity. This creates an inconvenience for the retailer, disrupts Saskatchewan and Manitoba markets, and puts upward pressure on prices paid to Alberta producers.

An Alberta "breaker" claimed that he was forced out of the eastern breaker markets by CEMA pricing practices. CEMA sets a Toronto-based price for surplus eggs and then adds a per-mile allowance for shipping. This breaker estimated that CEMA was allowing 2.25 cents per dozen eggs for transportation to the eastern market, while his actual costs were 6.75 cents per dozen.[5] As a consequence, he was now restricting his operations to Alberta.

---

[5] Although product moves in dried or frozen form, prices are still thought of in terms of equivalents of a dozen eggs.

TABLE 2-2
INITIAL PROVINCIAL SHARES OF THE NATIONAL EGG MARKET
(%)

British Columbia	12.055
Alberta	8.704
Saskatchewan	4.760
Manitoba	11.480
Ontario	38.161
Quebec	16.556
New Brunswick	1.828
Nova Scotia	4.106
P.E.I.	0.637
Newfoundland	1.785

Source: Federal-Provincial Comprehensive Marketing Program—Eggs.

Similar complaints about the rigidity of the pricing system were expressed in Saskatchewan, Manitoba and New Brunswick. A specific problem identified in Saskatchewan was the 7-cents-per-dozen price spread between Manitoba and Saskatchewan. Saskatchewan had traditionally imported a relatively small number of eggs from Manitoba, and a price level equivalent to the Manitoba price plus transportation prevailed. It is felt that the 7-cent differential established by CEMA does not reflect current transportation costs and that Saskatchewan producers are, therefore, not receiving as high a price for their production as they would if price differentials were established according to actual transportation costs rather than CEMA decree.

In Manitoba, one respondent was concerned about apparent pricing anomalies for eggs. The Toronto price for grade "A" eggs is 5 cents per dozen above the Manitoba price, while the Saskatchewan price is 7 cents above the Manitoba price. Since both these provinces are net importers of Manitoba eggs, the price differentials should reflect the cost of transporting eggs between these markets. The price differential of 7 cents and the distance of less than five hundred miles between the Manitoba and Saskatchewan markets is inconsistent with the 5-cent differential and the more than thousand-mile distance between the Manitoba and Toronto markets. It is apparent that price differentials do not reflect the actual cost of transportation between regions. The respondent expressed the opinion that differentials were set according to political rather than economic criteria.

In New Brunswick, a problem with CEMA's assumptions about trade flows was identified. While eggs normally flow from New Brunswick into Quebec and the price differentials between these two provinces reflect this pattern (Quebec prices are higher than N.B. prices), occasional or temporary shortages in New Brunswick cannot be accompanied by a price change that would encourage imports.

A problem cited by several persons interviewed was the rigidity of the provincial quotas set in the national market-sharing scheme. Reallocation of market shares between provinces can only take place for increases in quota above the level prevailing at initial allocation.[6] For the egg agency, reallocation was not an issue until recently because major reductions in aggregate quota levels were made after the agency commenced operation. When reallocation of quota becomes a possibility, changes in market shares will be difficult to obtain because gains for one province must be willingly given up by another province. Even the criteria by which negotiations are supposed to be guided are suspect. As one provincial government official put it: "Four of the five criteria by which market share reallocation are negotiated relate directly to provincial self-sufficiency in production." The criteria by which market share changes are to be negotiated are outlined in the relevant federal-provincial agreement. The criteria are: 1) the principle of comparative advantage of production; 2) any variation in the size of the market for eggs; 3) any failures by egg producers in any province or provinces to market the number of dozens of eggs authorized to be marketed; 4) the feasibility of increased production in each province; and 5) comparative transportation costs to market areas from alternative sources of production.

The feeling that national market-sharing schemes are "slanted" toward provincial self-sufficiency revealed itself in several statements. Said one official, "One or two exporting provinces will never have a chance against eight or nine provinces who see a chance to achieve self-sufficiency." Another stated, "Comparative advantage is just a motherhood statement. Determining comparative advantage is difficult and nobody really wants to use it in quota reallocation anyway."

---

[6] Initial allocation provided for a global reduction of the national production with quota being distributed pro rata amongst the provinces. This was done to lower production and increase prices. Since that time, production quotas have increased (pro rata) to nearly 100 per cent of the initial allocation. For increases in the national quota above 100 per cent of the initial allocation, individual provinces may attempt to negotiate higher market shares for themselves.

Licencing powers of the agency were also cited as an impediment to interprovincial trade. The federal-provincial agreement states:

> The agency shall . . . establish a system for the licensing of persons who are engaged in the marketing of eggs in interprovincial or export trade . . . prescribe the terms and conditions to which each license issued pursuant to the system is subject, including a condition that the person to whom the license is issued shall at all times during the term of such license comply with orders and regulations of the agency.

These comprehensive licencing powers were the basis for the sentiment that while there are no legal restrictions preventing product movement, it is easy for the agency to "discourage" unwanted movement.

The Canadian Chicken Marketing Agency

The Canadian Chicken Marketing Agency was established in 1978. All provinces except Alberta and Newfoundland are members. National production quotas are allocated to the provincial boards on a yearly and quarterly basis; the provincial boards in turn establish production quotas for individual producers. Pricing of chicken is the responsibility of individual provincial boards, a different system than with CEMA, which is much more involved in the pricing function. The allocation of shares of the national market for chickens follows essentially the same mechanisms as outlined for the egg marketing agency.

While the criteria by which renegotiation of market shares can take place are similar to those applicable to eggs, the emphasis is perhaps even more on the degree of provincial self-sufficiency. In any decision to reallocate quota, the agency must take into account: 1) any significant change in consumer demands; 2) the ability of any province to meet its allocated production; 3) the total market requirement within each market area; 4) the proportion of market demand in a province that is met by production in that province; and 5) the comparative advantage of production and marketing of chickens.

The licencing powers given to national agencies are of particular concern in the case of the Chicken Marketing Agency. The Canadian Chicken Licencing Regulations, made pursuant to the Farm Products Marketing Agencies Act, were passed in 1980 but have not yet been implemented. The regulations create potential barriers to interprovincial movement of live and processed chicken. The regulation states in section 4 as follows:

> No person shall engage in the marketing of chicken in interprovincial trade as a producer, producer-processor, processor, dealer or retailer unless he holds the appropriate licence set out in section nine and pays to the Agency annually the fee prescribed by that section for that licence.

23

The licences are restricted to those who have regularly engaged in interprovincial marketing of chicken over the five years preceding the promulgation of the regulations, and the amount of chicken that may be marketed is further limited to an authorized volume based on that individual's interprovincial marketing over the same period. The legislation is legally controversial, especially in Alberta where the provincial board believes that it was passed to "punish" Alberta producers for not joining the national agency. Certainly, the regulation is subject to interpretation and should the agency begin to implement it, the Alberta board states that it will launch court proceedings.

The Canadian Turkey Marketing Agency

The Canadian Turkey Marketing Agency was established in 1973 with all provinces except Prince Edward Island, New Brunswick and Newfoundland being party to the agreement. The CTMA is similar to the other national supply management marketing boards with regard to the establishment of national quota and its allocation between provinces. Pricing is the responsibility of the provincial boards in consultation with the CTMA. Again, concerns about rigidity of provincial production patterns, the "self-sufficiency" bias in market share renegotiation, and the possible effects of licencing powers apply to the turkey board as much as to the other boards.

The "trade war" background of these national agencies is evident in many parts of the legislation. For instance, the turkey agreement includes a section titled "anti-dumping," in which price discrimination between provincial markets is prohibited. Another example can be found in section 6 (II) of the chicken agreement, where one of the agency's policies is defined as: "not to increase the quota allocation of a province which engages in predatory marketing practices, including the shorting of an intraprovincial market so as to supply a market traditionally supplied by another province."

The actual or potential role of national supply management marketing agencies in influencing interprovincial trade flows was emphasized again and again in discussions with interested parties across Canada. The bias toward provincial self-sufficiency in quota allocation and reallocation procedures, and the licencing and other administrative powers of these agencies were considered the most serious threats to a "common market" for the commodities concerned. Many of those commenting on the agencies were careful to point out that these impediments to trade were the result of federal, not provincial, legislation.

The Canadian Wheat Board

The Canadian Wheat Board is unique in several respects. Unlike many other marketing boards whose objective is to manage domestic markets, the Wheat Board's mandate is, effectively, to manage export sales. While most marketing boards have a provincial constituency, the Canadian Wheat Board's constituency includes the entire Prairie region. While most marketing boards are controlled by producers using powers delegated by the provincial and federal governments, the Wheat Board is a federal Crown corporation with a producer advisory board.

The origins of the board can be traced to the creation of the Board of Grain Supervisors to cope with grain marketing problems that arose in 1917 and 1918. In 1919 the Board of Grain Supervisors was disbanded but was replaced almost immediately by the Canadian Wheat Board. The Wheat Board was disbanded after only one year of operation (1919) because the government felt that the special circumstances that prevailed during the war years no longer existed and that the pre-war marketing system should be reintroduced.

During the 1920s Prairie farmers developed strong grain-marketing cooperatives. These "Wheat Pools" were handling approximately 50 per cent of the grain marketed on the Prairies by the end of the 1920s. The world Depression created severe difficulties for the pools, leading to the re-establishment of the Canadian Wheat Board. The series of events has been described quite succinctly by Drummond, Anderson and Kerr in their review of agricultural policy in Canada:

> In early 1930 an emergency developed in connection with the marketing of wheat. The Wheat Pools had undertaken to make an initial payment to producers of $1 per bushel basis No. 1 Northern Fort William for the crop of 1929, to be financed as usual by the commercial banks on the security of warehousing receipts. At the start of the marketing year the Pools and the banks felt that the prospects of sales justified that initial payment. Within a few months the price of wheat fell until it approached the level of the initial payment, whereupon the banks requested additional collateral. The Pools sought aid from their respective provincial governments, which agreed to underwrite the loans. A few months later the price of wheat dropped to almost 50 cents per bushel and the Western interests appealed to the Federal government, which agreed to provide the banks with the necessary guarantee on condition that a government appointee become general manager of the Central Selling Agency of the Pools. With the appointment of McFarland to this position, the Federal government became actively involved in the marketing of wheat as it had been from 1917 – 19.
>
> The general policy followed by McFarland from 1930 to 1935 consisted in buying and holding wheat and wheat futures in order to support the current market price; it was anticipated that the amounts held off the

market could be disposed of later at prices high enough to prevent serious losses. In effect the government undertook a major five-year gamble in wheat prices because the forces affecting the market were beyond those with which the regular institutions of the trade could cope. Crop failures in the United States and Argentina in 1935, and a small crop in North America in 1936 made it possible for the government to win this gamble.[7]

In 1943 the Wheat Board was given exclusive control over the marketing of wheat, this extension of powers being brought about by special circumstances encountered in time of war. In 1948 the board's powers were further extended to include the marketing of barley and oats.

As the sole seller of grains produced in the "designated area" (Manitoba, Saskatchewan, Alberta, and the Peace River district of British Columbia), the board had considerable power in the domestic feed grains market. Interprovincial movement of grain was severely restricted in the sense that the Wheat Board was the *only* entity allowed to transport grain across provincial boundaries. In the extreme, this meant that an individual possessing a farm in Saskatchewan and a ranch in Alberta was not allowed to move feed grains from his farm to his ranch. Although the act clearly prevented grain producers from moving their product across provincial boundaries, the courts decided *(Murphy* v. *C.P.R.)* that there was no impediment to the interprovincial movement of grain, since the Wheat Board was willing and able to supply any demand for grain in any province.

Although the Wheat Board did not discriminate between provinces in terms of price, prices paid by livestock feeders in the intraprovincial markets of the Prairie provinces were substantially lower than prices paid by livestock producers in B.C. and Eastern Canada for "board" grains.

Livestock producers in Eastern Canada and B.C. felt that they were at a disadvantage compared to livestock producers within the designated area. The board's policy in pricing western feed grains was to set prices at Thunder Bay that would make the grains competitive with imported corn. Feed grains that could not be sold in the export or domestic markets by the board were stored on Prairie farms. At times, large stocks of feed grains accumulated, causing depressed prices in the intraprovincial markets in each of the Prairie provinces. Large price differentials were often observed between the "off board" price of feed

---

[7] W.M. Drummond, M.J. Anderson and T.C. Kerr, *A Review of Agricultural Policy in Canada* (Ottawa: Agricultural Economics Research Council of Canada, 1966), p. 38.

grains, which prevailed in the Prairie intraprovincial markets, and the board price, which prevailed in Eastern Canada and B.C.

These price differentials often exceeded those justifiable on the basis of transportation costs and were therefore not consistent with an open or national market for feed grains. Since the mid-1960s, there have been a number of changes that were designed to create equal access to Prairie feed grains for all market participants in Canada. The Canadian Livestock Feed Board was created in 1967 to provide a "countervailing power" to the Wheat Board. In 1973 and 1974 a new National Feed Grains Policy was introduced. The power to control the movement of feed grains between provinces was removed from the Wheat Board. Several other powers that could be used to influence movement of feed grains for domestic consumption, including the setting of delivery quotas and the allocation of transportation services, were also eliminated.

In a series of subsequent developments, the powers of the Wheat Board with regard to the marketing of domestic feed grains have changed several times:

- Feed grains for delivery to the domestic market were once again included in the Wheat Board delivery quota system. This had the effect of reintroducing a "separation" of the intraprovincial markets in the Prairie provinces and the markets outside of the Prairie provinces.
- The power to allocate transportation services was returned to the Wheat Board.
- The power to allocate transportation services was transferred from the Wheat Board to the newly created Grain Transportation Authority.

In a recent meeting with the minister of agriculture and the minister responsible for the Canadian Wheat Board, the board requested that it become, once again, the sole seller of feed grains for domestic consumption. If this request is granted, the flirtation with an open domestic feed grains market will have indeed been brief (six years). Even without returning pricing powers to the board, the openness of the domestic market has been seriously eroded by restrictions imposed by the reintroduction of delivery quotas and administrative allocation of transportation services.

Provincial Supply Management Marketing Boards

Many of the provincial supply management marketing boards have become a part of national marketing agencies because effective regulation of easily transportable commodities is extremely difficult without having control over interprovincial and international trade. The provincial fluid milk marketing boards are an exception. An important contributing factor in the boards' success has been the relative difficulty in transporting fluid milk.

Fluid milk production and marketing is controlled largely through provincial marketing boards, which may set prices and determine allocation of fluid milk quotas, as well as administer the industrial milk policies of the CDC. There is very little interprovincial movement of fluid milk other than to "border" cities. This lack of movement, historically, was due to the high perishability of fresh milk. Regulation of the industry was health oriented, and although transportation modes have now improved to permit the safe transport of milk for relatively long distances, the provincial regulations have been maintained to protect traditional markets.

The following are several representative examples of the type of regulation that restricts the interprovincial movement of fluid milk:

- In British Columbia, the B.C. Milk Industry Act requires that there be no sale of fluid milk except by *certified* dairy farms, and that a ministerial permit is required in order to transport fluid milk into the province. These permits, this study's researchers were informed, are "very difficult" to obtain. Milk prices in British Columbia, with the exception of Newfoundland, are the highest in Canada (prices and production quotas are set by the B.C. Milk Board). Due to the stringency of the regulations, less expensive Alberta fluid milk cannot be marketed in B.C. This is not to imply that Alberta dairies would wish to do away with these barriers, since they are similarly protected from eastern producers.

- The Ontario Milk Act (1965) provides the legislative basis for the regulation of fluid milk in Ontario. The Ontario Milk Marketing Board (OMMB), which enforces the act, regulates the production, processing and marketing of milk and milk products, and has an effective monopoly on the sale of raw milk in Ontario. The province is divided into regional milk distribution zones, and in order to sell milk in a zone, producers must have their facilities inspected by Ontario inspectors, and these inspectors do not travel outside the province.

  There are currently two fluid milk producers in Quebec who have Ontario permits for the Hawkesbury and Ottawa zones. The milk is sold through the OMMB but producers are paid Quebec prices.

  A major retailer indicated that because of geographical location and economy in distribution, the OMMB allows fluid milk processed in Winnipeg to be transported to centres in northwestern Ontario. However, the OMMB requires a reciprocal purchase of an equivalent amount of the raw product from the Ontario milk shed.

- A major retailer in Saskatchewan indicated that the retail trade was unable to import fluid milk products from other provinces because of the regulation of the Saskatchewan Milk Control Board. The retailer complained that a recent application to process fluid milk in the province had also been denied. Further, the opinion was expressed that the milk distribution zoning within the province reduces incentive to reinvest in milk processing and distribution facilities, resulting in outdated and inefficient operations.

- In 1980, UHT (ultra high temperature) milk was being produced in British Columbia, Alberta, Ontario and Quebec. Currently, the provinces are treating UHT milk as fluid milk, and thus interprovincial trade is highly restricted. This product is very similar to fluid milk from the consumer's point of view, but it is much more transportable and storable than fluid milk, having a shelf life of several weeks without refrigeration. Although the sales of UHT milk are still small (2-3 per cent of fluid milk sales), it has a good market growth potential. Current regulatory practices ensure that a major product advantage—low perishability when being transported—is not realized.

The methods of restricting the interprovincial movement of this product vary, but Ontario, for example, has used a multi-tiered approach. The Ontario Milk Act initially required that UHT milk be labelled "sterile." This was prior to Ontario developing a UHT milk industry but subsequent to the development of a Quebec UHT industry. According to Quebec government officials, this labelling requirement effectively barred the entry of the Quebec product until Ontario had developed its own industry, at which time the requirement was dropped. Currently, however, UHT milk in Ontario can be handled only by Ontario-licenced milk distributors, thus effectively barring Quebec sales of UHT milk products in Ontario.

Other Provincial Marketing Boards

Hog marketing is regulated by provincial marketing boards, but no effort is made to manage supply. At present, the Prairie provinces, Ontario and the Maritimes have active hog marketing boards. The major objectives of these boards are to ensure fair marketing of hogs, product promotion, and market development. The boards require that all hogs be marketed through a single agency, sometimes using special auction mechanisms. In this way, opportunities for buyers to engage in unfair marketing practices are reduced to a minimum, and producers can strengthen their bargaining power in the market. Like many other boards, the hog boards have been delegated powers over intraprovincial trade by their respective provincial governments and over interprovincial trade by the federal government. This gives the boards complete control over the marketing of hogs produced in their own province but does not allow them to regulate producers in other provinces. In the case of *Burns Food* v. *A.G. of Manitoba* (1974), it became clear that while a board could control the movement of all hogs produced in the province (including movement into export or interprovincial markets), it could not regulate the product entering from another province. This creates problems for some boards, and in some cases (involving commodities other than hogs) has resulted in countermeasures involving considerable imagination. At different times in Newfoundland and in B.C., regulations required that eggs produced outside the province but marketed within the province had to be individually stamped to identify them as "imports." These regulations were short-lived because they were almost immediately challenged and declared *ultra vires.*

More often potential problems in relation to interprovincial trade are dealt with through cooperation between boards in the various provinces or through the use of moral suasion. It is not unusual for processors or retailers to favour local producers even when no pressure to do so is present. For commodities such as eggs and fresh vegetables, the added freshness associated with local supplies is important to buyers. Dealing with local suppliers also helps to maintain a firm's favourable image and has a good public relations value. Buyers are also often reluctant to take a "deal" on imported products, preferring to maintain good relations with reliable local suppliers. Several people involved in egg marketing indicated that locally produced eggs can usually command a two to three cent per dozen premium over "imported" eggs.

Many of the people interviewed acknowledged the role of moral suasion in the operations of marketing boards, but only isolated cases were cited as having unduly restricted interprovincial trade.

Subsidies and Other Government Assistance

Discussions with academics, government officials, and people in the private sector about barriers to interprovincial trade often included mention of the problem of differences between provinces and/or regions in terms of government assistance to the agricultural and food-processing sectors. Many persons interviewed felt that this was one of the major factors distorting interprovincial trade patterns. Three major areas of concern were mentioned in this regard: federal agricultural policies with a regional emphasis; the activities of the federal Department of Regional Economic Expansion; and the agricultural policies of provincial governments.

Federal Agricultural Policies with a Regional Emphasis

The federal agricultural policies that generated the most concern with regard to trade distortion were the National Feed Grains Policy, regulation of the Prairie grain industry by the Canadian Wheat Board, statutory rail freight rates for the movement of Prairie grains into export positions, and transportation subsidies. These issues have already been dealt with in this study.

Activities of the Department of Regional Economic Expansion

The objective of the Department of Regional Economic Expansion (DREE) is to assist each region of Canada to realize its economic and social potential. This goal is pursued by providing incentives for industrial expansion in specific regions. To the extent that DREE is successful in diverting economic activity into regions where it would not otherwise have located, the department's activities can be considered a deliberate attempt to distort trade patterns or otherwise decrease the degree of economic integration in the national economy. Although this may have some undesirable economic effects, important social, cultural or political objectives can be achieved, and regional development is generally considered an important element of national policy.

An indication of the regional distribution of the department's activities can be seen in per capita expenditure for each of the provinces (see Table 3-1).

TABLE 3-1
DREE EXPENDITURES, 1978-79
($'s per capita)

Newfoundland	108.16
Nova Scotia	62.59
Prince Edward Island	248.65
New Brunswick	75.45
Quebec	27.35
Ontario	2.66
Manitoba	27.48
Saskatchewan	48.24
Alberta	8.73
British Columbia	6.11

Source: Department of Regional Economic Expansion, *Annual Report, 1978–1979* (Ottawa: 1980).

Agriculture is only one of many sectors of the economy to which DREE programs apply. Fisheries, forestry, tourism, urban development, mining and minerals, infrastructure, and industrial development are also important areas in which DREE is active.

Although the concept of regional incentives was questioned by some, the most severe criticism was directed at the way in which the department carried out its programs. Specifically, it was felt that the department did not adequately evaluate the impact of its programs on economic activity in other regions. The British Columbia Select Standing Committee on Agriculture made some particularly strong statements in its report on DREE activity in Western Canada's food industry:

> This study established that the frozen french fry potato processing industry, based on normal industry operation, is currently overbuilt by approximately 60%. It is significant to note that RDIA [Regional Development Incentives Act, administered by the federal Department of Regional Economic Expansion] grants have supported the construction of potato processing plants in New Brunswick, P.E.I., Manitoba and Swan Valley in B.C. The overcapacity fostered by RDIA grants has been largely responsible for the closure of one plant in Ontario and Spetifore Frozen Foods in B.C. and the possible future closure of potato processing by Fresh Pak in

British Columbia. This report has termed DREE's actions in supporting the McCains plant at Portage La Prairie at best naive and at worst, irresponsible.

The analysis undertaken in this study also determined that DREE activities in the beef industry in Alberta promoted a situation of over-capacity which was a significant factor in the closure of 2 plants in Alberta and 3 plants in British Columbia.

Our analysis of the RDIA program has determined that the major reason for this critical situation is DREE's inadequate management of its funding, and insufficient evaluation of its applications.[1]

DREE, in association with the Quebec provincial government, has been particularly active in allocating financial aid to the Quebec dairy industry in recent years. The massive, farmer-owned Granby Co-operative was the recipient of over $10 million from these two sources for the building of new processing facilities in the late 1970s. Needless to say, processors in Ontario took a dyspeptic view of this use of government funds, as it serves to erode their market position in the national cheese market.

Agricultural Policies of Provincial Governments

The federal government and the provinces have concurrent jurisdiction in agriculture (section 95, BNA Act). While the federal jurisdiction predominates in this area, agriculture has traditionally been an area of strong provincial involvement. The federal government's role has emphasized basic research, the interprovincial and international aspects of agriculture such as grades and standards, transfer payments such as the industrial milk subsidy, various transportation subsidies, and stabilization plans.

In several other areas, there has been a good deal of cooperation and coordination between the federal and provincial governments. Both levels of government are involved in providing assistance in the area of agricultural credit. Crop insurance involves a cost-sharing agreement between the federal and provincial governments. In other areas, such as extension and rural development and adjustment, government involvement has been almost exclusively at the provincial level.

One method that has been used to illustrate differences between provinces with regard to the extent of government assistance is to compare direct transfer payments (cash subsidies) to farmers with total farm cash receipts. The relevant data is presented in Table 3-2.

Such a comparison is misleading in some respects, since many of the

---

[1] British Columbia Select Standing Committee on Agriculture, *The Impact of the Department of Regional Economic Expansion on the Food Industry in Western Canada* (May 1978), pp. vi-vii.

transfers are product specific. For instance, the reason Quebec has the "most-subsidized" agriculture in many of the years tabulated is related to federal dairy subsidies. Dairy subsidies apply equally to all industrial milk producers in Canada. The preponderance of production in the province of Quebec accounts for the size of the transfers to farmers in that province. Quebec has not always held the most-subsidized position. In 1970 Saskatchewan took first place as a result of payments under the program Lower Inventory for Tomorrow, designed to reduce burdensome inventories of wheat and other grains. In 1975 Prince Edward Island and New Brunswick were contenders for first place because of deficiency payments on potatoes. B.C.'s agriculture was the most subsidized in 1976 as a result of substantial payments under the provincial stabilization plan in that year.

Provincial involvement in stabilization schemes is a relatively recent phenomenon. British Columbia was the first to implement a plan, but all of the other provinces have become involved to varying degrees. A brief summary follows of the plans that have operated within the last five years or that are in operation at present. (A more detailed description of the various provincial schemes can be found in Appendix B.)

- British Columbia: A stabilization plan to which participating producers and the provincial government contribute equally.
- Alberta: A stabilization plan for hogs funded entirely by the provincial government. A program of assistance to feeder calf producers was effective in 1977.
- Saskatchewan: A stabilization plan for hogs to which participating producers and the provincial government contribute equally. A program of assistance to feeder calf producers was effective in 1975—77.
- Manitoba: A plan involving support prices for feeder calves and slaughter cattle. Producers pay into the plan when market prices are above the support price and receive payments when market prices are below the support price.
- Ontario: A stabilization plan for feeder calves. The provincial government contributes two dollars for each dollar paid into the plan by producers.
- Quebec: A stabilization plan involving contributions by producers (one-third) and the provincial government (two-thirds). Covered products include weanling pigs, feeder calves, slaughter cattle, potatoes and several grains.
- Nova Scotia, P.E.I., New Brunswick: Similar stabilization plans for hogs, including shared costs between producers and the provincial governments.

TABLE 3-2
FEDERAL AND PROVINCIAL GOVERNMENT DIRECT PAYMENTS TO PRODUCERS AS A PERCENTAGE OF FARM CASH RECEIPTS, 1968 – 79

Province	1968	1969	1970	1971	1972	1973	1974	1975	1976	1977	1978	1979
Prince Edward Island	7.4	3.9	2.7	3.6	5.3	2.9	3.7	11.0	3.6	4.9	7.4	7.0
Nova Scotia	1.2	0.6	0.4	.5	1.0	0.3	1.4	2.2	3.3	2.6	2.1	2.5
New Brunswick	3.4	3.2	1.4	1.5	3.5	1.1	1.6	6.4	1.9	2.2	4.2	4.0
Quebec	7.6	5.9	4.4	7.5	7.7	7.2	11.8	11.7	9.6	9.6	7.6	7.0
Ontario	2.8	2.3	1.6	2.3	2.9	2.0	3.0	4.2	4.0	4.1	2.5	3.0
Manitoba	1.7	1.6	2.9	2.5	3.3	2.4	1.2	2.3	3.3	2.4	1.2	0.8
Saskatchewan	1.2	1.3	5.5	1.1	3.1	2.5	1.1	0.3	0.7	1.5	0.6	0.2
Alberta	1.8	1.9	3.2	1.6	3.4	2.7	3.2	1.0	1.1	3.7	1.3	0.6
British Columbia	0.9	0.4	0.6	0.2	0.5	1.4	5.7	5.8	9.8	8.9	4.6	1.8

Source: Statistics Canada, *Farm Cash Receipts*, various issues.

35

Many of these programs are so new that payments to farmers have not been made under some plans (or for some commodities within a plan). Nevertheless, a review of expenditures up to the end of 1979 is informative (see Table 3-3).

TABLE 3-3
PAYMENTS OUT OF PROVINCIAL STABILIZATION SCHEMES
AS A PERCENTAGE OF FARM CASH RECEIPTS, 1973 – 79

Province	1973	1974	1975	1976	1977	1978	1979
Quebec	–	–	–	–	0.3	0.4	–
Ontario	–	–	0.9	0.8	0.4	–	0.2
Manitoba	–	–	1.0	2.2	0.8	–	–
Saskatchewan	–	–	–	0.4	1.0	–	–
Alberta	–	–	–	–	2.1	–	–
British Columbia	0.6	4.0	3.8	6.7	6.5	3.0	0.6

Note: No payments were reported for the provinces of Newfoundland, Nova Scotia, New Brunswick or Prince Edward Island.

Source: Statistics Canada, *Farm Cash Receipts*, various issues.

British Columbia was the first province to establish a provincially sponsored agricultural stabilization plan. It remains the most comprehensive plan and has resulted in substantial payments to producers, peaking at 6.7 per cent of farm cash receipts in 1976. Provincial stabilization programs in the Prairie provinces and in Ontario have so far been restricted largely to measures to help beef cow-calf operators through the particularly difficult times from 1975 to 1977. Payments made under the Quebec plan have thus far been quite modest. While provincial hog stabilization plans are in place in P.E.I., Nova Scotia and New Brunswick, there have apparently not been any payments under these plans as of the end of 1979.

Stabilization schemes, although the most highly visible of measures, are not the only method by which provincial governments assist agricultural production. Another important measure that leads to variation between provinces in terms of government assistance is related to capital formation through subsidized interest on borrowings, loan guarantees, or capital grants. Some specific examples are:

● Newfoundland: 1) grants for up to 25 per cent of the capital construction cost of on-farm vegetable storage, maximum $10,000; 2) low-interest government loans for purchase of livestock, machinery or buildings.

- Nova Scotia: 1) grants up to 50 per cent of the capital cost of on-farm feed storage and processing facilities, maximum $12,000. Similar programs for hogs (25 per cent/$20,000) and greenhouse production (25 per cent/ $70,000); 2) grants for capital expenditure related to farm buildings, maximum $8,000 per year.

- New Brunswick: 1) financial assistance for establishment and maintenance of apple orchards, $650 per acre plus $1 per tree; 2) subsidy to offset interest paid on Farm Credit Corporation loans; 3) livestock purchase assistance: guaranteed loans, 20 per cent can become a grant if certain conditions are met.

- Prince Edward Island: 1) grants up to 50 per cent of capital costs related to farm buildings or equipment, maximum $25,000; 2) grants for construction of on-farm grain storage facilities; 3) Prince Edward Island is nearing the end of a fifteen-year (1969–84) comprehensive agricultural development plan. The plan emphasized development of the potato industry through capital grants for storage facilities and equipment. Although this program is distinctly provincial in thrust, it is almost entirely federally funded.

- Quebec: 1) grants toward capital cost of grain storage facilities; 2) financial incentives to rationalize dairy- and meat-processing sectors; 3) grants toward capital cost of beef feedlot construction ($100 per head capacity, maximum $40,000).

- Ontario: government loans at 6 per cent interest for up to 75 per cent of cost of tile drainage installation.

- Manitoba: government loans and guarantees to assist financing of agricultural production, maximum $60,000.

- Saskatchewan: "Farmstart," grants and/or low interest loans to encourage viable units and/or diversification of agricultural production.

- Alberta: 1) loan guarantees for agribusiness firms;

	2) government loans for farm development; rebates on principal provide incentives in the dairy and vegetable sectors.
● British Columbia:	1) financial assistance for the agricultural inputs and processing sectors; 2) farm loan guarantees and interest subsidy.

Another source of variation between provinces is in the area of direct subsidies. Although activity in this area is limited, there are a few worthy of note: Nova Scotia pays $100 per head for female beef breeding stock added to existing herds (maximum of 50 per cent expansion/50 females); Nova Scotia pays a subsidy of $1.50/cwt. on industrial milk production; and Quebec pays a direct subsidy of from $20 to $45 per head (depending on herd size) for over-wintering beef cattle.

Almost all provincial governments are involved in several other policy areas. These are apparently more consistent between provinces because no specific comments were made on them during interviews. Some examples are land reclamation/improvement assistance, assistance to agricultural associations, livestock/crop breed improvement incentives, assistance relating to soil fertility improvement, farm management assistance, and social programs (for example, 4-H). Other programs, such as crop insurance and the small farms development program, are relatively consistent between provinces because of the participation of the federal government.

While no comments on specific programs in these areas were made, more than one person interviewed indicated that their effective use varied between provinces. Quebec in particular was viewed as "aggressive" or as having "gotten good mileage" out of its programs through initiative in, and cooperation between, the government and agricultural sectors.

Specific concerns aired during the interviews quite naturally tended to be commodity and/or region specific. In Atlantic Canada, for instance, Nova Scotia's incentives to increase livestock production were considered "rich" by producers in neighbouring provinces. Maritime potato producers expressed concern about developments relating to Quebec's potato industry. Hog producers in the Prairie provinces (especially in Alberta) have expressed concerns about the massive shift of pork production for the Prairies into Quebec and British Columbia and about the role provincial policies in these provinces have played in encouraging that shift.

Other Policies and Regulations

4

Provincial Procurement Policies

All provinces exercise government procurement policies, both implicit and explicit, designed to give preferential treatment to provincially grown or manufactured products. In order to identify these preferences, it is necessary in some provinces to contact the purchasing department in every provincial department, agency, board or institution, since these preferences stem generally from purchasing policies and not from law. Thus, as an interprovincial barrier to trade, these policies are frequently difficult to identify.

The federal government, in a discussion paper entitled "Powers Over the Economy: Securing the Canadian Economic Union in the Constitution" published in July 1980, defines three ways in which preferences can be given on a government purchase:

> 1) *Requirements Definition.* Governments often set their own performance requirements for items they buy. If those standards are tailored closely and exclusively to the capabilities of firms within the province, this could constitute an interprovincial non-tariff barrier to trade.
> 2) *Sourcing Policy.* Most governments maintain source lists of producers who can supply wanted commodities. To the extent that firms outside a province have more difficulty getting on such lists than firms inside, or are not invited to tender, this constitutes a form of preference.
> 3) *Tender Evaluation.* Conceptually, preferences are easiest to spot and measure at this stage. If an in-province bid for some commodity is accepted despite it being higher than an outside province bid, the magnitude of the preference might be deemed to be the difference between the two.

This paper also sets forth, in point form, a summary of explicit provincial preferences identified. This listing, reproduced on the following page, is not exhaustive, and is of general application, since it does not focus on food and agricultural products, but it does indicate the thrust of several of the provinces' purchasing policies.

British Columbia	– "committed" to provincial preference
	– maximum premium of 10 per cent based on provincial content
Saskatchewan	– generally buy-Saskatchewan when all other factors are equal
	– limited number of products are restricted to in-province sources (Cabinet policy)
	– small premium paid on special occasions to buy-Saskatchewan
Quebec	– when sufficient competition exists, only Quebec enterprises are invited to tender
	– in exceptional cases, the above can be applied even without sufficient competition if it serves industrial development objectives
	– for contracts exceeding $50,000, a preference of up to 10 per cent is applied to the Quebec content of bids
	– tenders must state the percentages of Quebec, Canadian and foreign content
Nova Scotia	– Government Purchasing Act (1964) states wherever possible Nova Scotia products should be purchased and purchases should be from persons who maintain and operate businesses in the province
	– if at least three Nova Scotia suppliers are available, tenders are restricted to the province
	– even if less than three, tendering can be limited if Nova Scotia suppliers are reasonably competitive
	– up to 10 per cent premium in favour of Nova Scotia business, on an ad hoc basis to maintain particular industries
New Brunswick	– new policy based on New Brunswick content (October 1977) now being monitored
	– tenders are routinely evaluated both by cost and likely impact on New Brunswick employment and economy
	– information is demanded on all out-of-province sub-contracting and reasons therefore
	– sourcing limited to New Brunswick suppliers if three or more available
	– if nature of government demand warrants, New Brunswick sources can be developed through initial "cost plus" contracts, or product development assistance
Newfoundland	– Department of Public Works and Service Act states, wherever possible, Newfoundland products should be purchased and purchases should

be from persons who maintain and operate businesses in the province
— premiums of up to 10 per cent[1] are allowed in respect of products wholly or mainly, manufactured, grown or produced in the province

As well, provinces normally encourage local governments, hospitals and universities under their jurisdiction to follow the provincial government practices. When these institutions do not buy local products, producers can apply lobby pressure. For example, the city of Vancouver municipal offices were recently picketed by the provincial Bakers Association for purchasing buns from the United States (although the local product was 5 per cent more expensive than the foreign product).

Some provinces exercise different levels of preference. For example, Quebec policies reveal three different levels of preference: provincial, Canadian and foreign. The Ontario government provides a 10 per cent Canadian preference, while a provincial preference is occasionally exercised.[2]

Provincial governments are substantial consumers of goods and services and as such are capable of influencing economic activity within the province by favouring local suppliers in their procurement activities. Preferential procurement policies range from the obvious (up to 10 per cent provincial pricing advantage on a contract tender relative to an out-of-province supplier) to the subtle (inclusion of performance requirements that only local firms can meet). As well, the preferences exist at various levels of government and government-related/supported institutions. Consequently, quantification of such policies in terms of interprovincial barriers to the movement of food and agricultural products is most difficult.

Provincial Food and Agricultural Promotional Programs

The current provincial thrust for self-sufficiency manifests itself most visibly in the various provincial food and agricultural promotional programs. These programs are of differing magnitude and effect; the former being relatively easy to measure, the latter more subtle. Although the programs are ostensibly aimed at increasing consumption of

---

[1] Very recently, this provincial 10 per cent preference has been replaced with a policy based on the value-added concept, which takes into account provincial labour content and the use of Newfoundland resources.

[2] A.E. Safarian, *Ten Markets or One? Regional Barriers to Economic Activity in Canada* (Toronto: Ontario Economic Council, 1980).

local produce at the expense of foreign imports, if effective, such promotion has an impact on the volume of products imported from other provinces as well. A fruit and vegetable retailer, responding to moral suasion on the part of the provincial Department of Agriculture to carry local produce, to display the logo of the provincial program, and to advertise sales of the produce in conjunction with the logo, must have sufficient stock to supply customers responding to the advertisement. Inevitably, this reduces the likelihood of the retailer stocking an imported product, whether from foreign or other provincial sources. Of course, these programs merely institutionalize an inclination generally felt by processors and retailers to deal with local producers—for reasons of freshness, personal contacts, convenience and public relations. The public relations rationale is particularly important with regard to certain products of a "sensitive" nature (that is, chicken, eggs, potatoes, B.C. fresh fruit) in that a retailer must be very careful that there is no local source of supply before purchasing from outside the province.

The most developed program in Canada is that of the Ontario Ministry of Agriculture and Food, entitled Foodland Ontario. The program has an annual budget (1979) of $2 million and comprises a media advertising campaign, billboards, mall posters, exhibits, cost-sharing grants to Ontario commodity groups and marketing boards. As well, the retail and food services sectors are encouraged to carry Ontario produce and use the Foodland Ontario logo and slogan, "Good Things Grow in Ontario."

In Quebec the programs to promote Quebec agriculture are fragmented, with fresh produce under a program entitled l'Aide de Production des Produits Agricole, which has a budget of $500,000 a year. Again, advertising campaigns exhort Quebecers to buy Quebec produce, and producer groups may obtain dollar for dollar financing of promotional campaigns. Promotion of Quebec broilers under a marketing program named Becdor, according to a large New Brunswick processor, *does* make it more difficult to market out-of-province broilers.

British Columbia's marketing program has a budget of $150,000 (1979), with a logo and slogan, "Home Grown B.C. Quality." The minister of agriculture in B.C. recently stated that the province was aiming for 65 per cent self-sufficiency in food (currently it is 42 per cent) in the coming years, an unrealistic figure according to some agricultural observers.

The Saskatchewan Department of Agriculture encourages the sale and consumption of agricultural products, with a promotional budget of $60,000 per year. A Saskatchewan government official commented, rather sardonically, that the program, called Saskatchewan's Own, used a British Columbia advertising firm to create the advertisements, which were filmed in Winnipeg, and was supported by promotional ties and handkerchiefs purchased in Ontario and promotional books of matches purchased in Montreal!

The Maritime provinces, through a private program entitled Atlantic Canada Plus, promote all Maritime products. Emphasis in the program is on food and agricultural products, since studies indicated that a thrust in this direction would produce the greatest positive results (currently only 20 per cent of the food consumed in the Maritimes is produced there). Funding of the program in 1979 was 50 per cent private (memberships are sold), 25 per cent provincial government (Council of Maritime Premiers), and 25 per cent federal (Industry Trade and Commerce) as part of their " Shop Canadian" campaign. The total budget in 1979 was $400,000, and it was estimated that the 1980 budget would be approximately the same.

Both Manitoba and Newfoundland privately promote local produce through marketing boards (with some government support).

A private association called the Fresh for Flavour Foundation acts as the promotional arm for the Canadian Horticultural Council and Canadian Fruit Wholesalers Association. This foundation is regionalized throughout Canada and promotes, through advertising campaigns, a policy of "regional produce first, Canada second, and foreign third!" Foreign produce is promoted as well, but only during the off-season for competing produce in Canada.

Provincial food and agricultural promotion programs exist in all provinces or regions to various extents and clearly manifest the current provincial emphasis on self-sufficiency. Although the budgets vary from the modest annual expenditure of approximately $60,000 for the Saskatchewan's Own program, to several million dollars for Foodland Ontario, the intent is clear—*sell ours first*. This is accepted by all of the provinces, who each year meet to discuss their respective programs. To measure the impact of these programs on the free movement of food and agricultural products across Canada is most difficult, but without a doubt the programs serve to increase the competitive advantage of the local product vis-à-vis "imported" products. Of course, product differentiation is a common and well-accepted merchandising technique in all fields, particularly in the packaged-goods area. Differentiation of product by region is simply one facet of the general technique of product differentiation.

Liquor Control Regulation

The provinces regulate the marketing and distribution of alcoholic beverages, a commodity group (of which the sub-group of wines is particularly pertinent) that provides striking examples of multi-tiered barriers erected to protect local industry. These barriers are manifested as specific provincial production formulae, pricing practices and listing and distribution policies, both formal and informal, and are sufficiently restrictive to have been the cause of at least one complaint to GATT (General Agreement on Tariffs and Trade) by an exporting country. Wine, spirits and beer are all protected to varying degrees in relation to regional economic conditions.

In Ontario the barriers with regard to wines begin with the grape. The Liquor Control Act requires that Ontario wineries use only Ontario grapes, with the exception provided in the Wine Content Act. This act has permitted, for the period 1976 – 81, importation of grapes, juice or wine in amounts not exceeding 15 per cent of domestic production. No individual product, however, may contain more than 30 per cent imported material. This exception was permitted due to a shortage of white wine grapes in the mid-1970s; five years was considered an adequate time-period for the local industry to become self-sufficient in marketable white wine grapes. There are currently ten wineries in Ontario, with wine distribution through the Liquor Control Board of Ontario or through each winery's own retail outlets, of which there are currently 123. These outlets may sell only those products produced by the winery and listed with the Liquor Board. Wines produced out of the province must be sold through the Liquor Board.

In order to list with the Liquor Board, a winery must make an application and submit a sample. The merit of the application and sample will be considered by a listing committee on the following six criteria: quality; price; public demand; marketability; relationship to other products of the same type already listed by the board; and performance in other markets. The board admits that as a matter of policy every Ontario submission of adequate quality in the proper price range is listed, while imported wines are subjected to the full rigorous evaluation on all six criteria. In addition, Ontario wines can be merchandised in a wider range of bottle sizes than extra-provincial and imported wines.

Wine from outside the province is distributed exclusively through Ontario Liquor Control Board stores, of which there are about six hundred. Each store has a volume rating (A,B,C . . .), and listing in the store is under the authority of the store manager. An unwritten policy again favours Ontario wines in that they automatically achieve distribution through "A" and "B" stores, while all other wines must "sell" the store manager.

The next tier of protection for Ontario wines is in the markup. Tax on imported wine is 123 per cent, on other Canadian wine 105 per cent, and on Ontario wine 58 per cent (table, sparkling) and 75 per cent (dessert).

The sale of alcoholic spirits also reflects an Ontario bias, but only in markup rates that are lower for Ontario products; the rules for distribution do not discriminate against extra-provincial and imported products.

British Columbia also erects substantial barriers to protect their local wine industry. Wineries are permitted to import up to 20 per cent of their local crush, such percentage fluctuating with supply and demand. However, cottage wineries must use 100 per cent B.C.-grown grapes. Listing is automatic for B.C. wineries (limit of sixty-six selections per company), unlike Ontario; foreign wines must satisfy listing requirements much like those in Ontario.

Distribution for extra-provincial wines must commence in the regional stores that serve as a test market for eighteen months. If the wine reaches a fixed quota of sales, it is eligible for full distribution. B.C. wines are immediately eligible for full distribution and, as well, may test market their products in their own stores (located at the winery site).

There is a 46 per cent markup for B.C. wines, 100 per cent for all imports, Canadian and foreign.

A new form of restriction was implemented by the Liquor Control and Licencing Branch in January 1980 whereby Circular 210 required that restaurants in British Columbia list B.C. wines and feature them as house wines. The following is an extract from Circular 210:

> It is the policy of this Branch that all licensees carry a selection of British Columbia wines. As a minimum, licensees should carry at least one product in each category: white, red and rose. Sparkling and champagne type products are optional. All products should be referred to by company and/or product name as opposed to the general statement "B.C. Red, B.C. White, Canadian Wines," etc. It is important that the customer have the opportunity to select a product by company and/or brand name from the licensee's wine list.
>
> In addition, licensees should feature British Columbia wine as their "house" wine as an alternative to bottled selections. The house wine should *not* be referred to as B.C. Red, B.C. White, etc. but instead should be identified by company and/or product name. Where licensees choose to identify product by country, or where licensees choose to list domestic and imported wines separately, it is suggested that wine produced in British Columbia be featured under a heading "Wines of British Columbia."

This circular also regulates the specifications of "approved" carafes that house wines must be served in and requires that these carafes be purchased from named distributors supplied by a specified B.C. manufacturer.

Quebec approaches the marketing of wines from a different perspective in that the Quebec Liquor Commission (SAQ) itself bottles imported wines and provides the major competition for local wineries. Markups vary for wines by source of origin (wines from France have the lowest tariff rates), and distribution is through liquor stores and independent grocery stores. These grocery stores may sell only Quebec wines and SAQ bottled wine, and the proportionate representations and displays are all regulated by the SAQ.

Provincial liquor licencing legislation also regulates the distribution and sale of beer in Canada. In each province (other than P.E.I., which has no breweries), beer, in order to be sold at the lowest price to the consumer, must be brewed in the province. The Canadian Brewers Association estimates that 98 per cent of beer sold is brewed in the province of sale, with 2 per cent moving interprovincially.

To supply isolated regions, New Brunswick and Nova Scotia also sell beer "imported" from the sister province with the same markup as locally produced beer to maximize efficiencies in a small market. Other than these exceptions, if a brewery wishes to export to another province, the beer is treated as "imported" and marked up accordingly.

The marketing and distribution of alcoholic beverages (particularly wines) represent a very clear and unapologetic barrier to the interprovincial movement of these products. The primary wine-producing provinces of British Columbia, Ontario and Quebec provide the most striking examples of barriers that virtually prohibit the sale of out-of-province Canadian wines. When possible, wineries are required to use local grapes exclusively. Liquor store policies with regard to listings (brands made available in liquor stores) and markups favour local products over those imported from other provinces or countries. The barriers are not subtle; the protectionist policies are rationalized through attitudes such as "they're doing it to us, so we must do it to them"—a viewpoint that would not likely be endorsed by the wine consumer!

Packaging and Labelling

The federal Consumer Packaging and Labelling Act (CPL) and Regulations establish numerous packaging and labelling requirements for all packaged and pre-packaged products sold in Canada, and are the superceding legislation in this field. Other federal legislation, such as the Canada Agricultural Products Standards Act (CAPS) and Regulations, Meat Inspection Act/Regulations, Fish Inspection Act/Regulations, also contains packaging and labelling provisions specific to the products within the ambit of the legislation, but these provisions are enforceable only for items traded interprovincially and are almost identical to the Consumer Packaging and Labelling Act requirements.

Intraprovincial trade is the domain of the provincial legislatures, which have passed legislation also containing packaging and labelling provisions. Generally, the provincial legislation is equivalent to the federal, adopting the minimum CPL Act requirements, but it is within the jurisdiction of the provinces to add on additional requirements, or enact new requirements with regard to products not encompassed in federal legislation. Interprovincial barriers can be created by these "add ons" and by provisions specific to the provinces, as examples below will indicate.

The Consumer Fraud Protection Branch of Consumer and Corporate Affairs Canada enforces the federal legislation and most of the provincial legislation (at the request of the provinces), primarily at the retail level. This enforcement of provincial regulations is flexible. If the province is in short supply of a product, they may instruct the federal inspectors not to be too strict with regard to the labelling regulation in question, and the opposite pertains at times of oversupply.

Generally, packaging and labelling were not found to be barriers, but there were some exceptions:

- Butter wrap (foil versus parchment): The degree of opacity of the wrapping that butter is sold in is regulated both federally and provincially. At a meeting of the provinces and the federal government several years ago, it was agreed that butter should be sold in a wrapping that did not expose it to light. At that time, the provinces permitted butter to be wrapped in parchment of a transparent nature. After the meeting, the Quebec government immediately drafted legislation requiring that the butter be effectively foil wrapped. The other provinces did not follow suit, although the federal government promulgated identical legislation (Dairy Products Regulations – CAPS Act) applicable to interprovincial trade but not enforceable until 1 April 1981. Ontario has not yet passed such legislation and still permits butter to be sold in parchment wrap; thus Ontario cannot sell in the Quebec market (unless the producer wishes to use the more expensive foil wrap for Quebec markets). British Columbia, although it does not require foil wrap, has adopted this wrap as a trade practice. This barrier is erected, therefore, as a consequence of the provinces and federal government moving at different speeds in the same legislative direction.

- Bottling legislation: The provinces have jurisdiction over soft drink bottles (other than the safety feature), and due to different provincial environmental perspectives, the use of cans versus non-returnable soft drink containers is not consistent throughout the country. For example, Ontario permits both disposable and returnable soft drink containers, while Alberta and Saskatchewan permit only returnable containers. Since there are bottling plants in almost every province, retailers do not perceive this as a major barrier.

- Quebec language legislation: The federal Consumer Packaging and Labelling Act requires that all labels be in both official languages, English and French. The Quebec Charter of the French Language (Bill 101) states that all labelling must be in French, and if in French and another language, then the French must be as prominent as the other language. This legislation, although its legality is still being contested, has created a barrier to those manufacturers and processors who wish to sell in Quebec, since they must re-label all items to comply with the Quebec standard. Enforcement of the Quebec legislation is uneven. The federal consumer fraud inspectors have been instructed to warn vendors of products with French-only labelling (in contravention of the Consumer Packaging and Labelling Act) but not to seize these products, while the Quebec government actively prosecutes any party labelling with English only.

Grades, Standards and Their Enforcement

The overlapping federal and provincial jurisdictions over grades and standards, and the complexity of enforcement practices have created a multitude of past, current and potential interprovincial barriers for food and agricultural products. The federal Food and Drug Act and Regulations are the overriding federal legislation with regard to consumer health protection and economic fraud in the manufacture and sale of foods (*inter alia*). Their jurisdiction extends to food offered for sale throughout Canada, both inter- and intraprovincially, in contrast with the CAPS Act and Meat Inspection Act, for example, which have merely interprovincial and export/import jurisdiction. The Food and Drug Act and Regulations prescribe standards of composition for a wide variety of food products. The CAPS Act and Regulations prescribe grades and standards for processed and fresh fruit and vegetable products, dairy products and other agricultural commodities. The Meat Inspection Act and Regulations require that all meats destined for interprovincial movement be federally inspected and stamped with the "Canada" meat legend.

Provincial agricultural legislation, such as the Farm Products Grades and Sales Act (Ontario) and Loi sur les Produits Agricoles et les Aliments (Quebec), also prescribes grades and standards for most agricultural products, such grades and standards being for the most part identical to the federal legislation. Where there are exceptions, there arise barriers to trade, as will be set forth below.

The enforcement of grades and standards can create barriers; it is inconsistent with regard to certain commodities and is highly subject to fluctuations of provincial surpluses and thus to political (in the broadest sense) interference. For example, no federal certificate is required for interprovincial trade of fresh fruits and vegetables under the CAPS Act/Regulations (unlike processed fruits and vegetables). Inspection is not legislated for this fresh produce—the product must be "Canada" grade, but it may be graded by federal or provincial inspectors, or none at all, depending upon agreements between the provinces and the federal government. Specific examples of barriers created by the inspection structure will be discussed below.

A landmark Supreme Court of Canada decision in December 1979 called into question the federal authority to pass regulations regarding the prescription of standards of composition. In *Labatt Breweries of Canada Limited* v. *The Queen et al* (30, 1980 N.R., 469), the constitutional validity of the Food and Drug Act standard for light beer was tested. The appellant had marketed a "light beer" in violation (so found) of the "light beer" standard in the Food and Drug Regulations, and the Court held, in the most narrow sense, that the prescription of standards was *ultra vires* the Parliament of Canada insofar as they related to malt liquors. Generalized, this decision renders invalid all federal standards insofar as they relate to intraprovincial trade. In the same month, the Supreme Court of Canada in *Dominion Stores* v. *The Queen et al* (30, 1980 N.R., 399) questioned the constitutional validity of Part 1 of the CAPS Act with regard to the retail sale of graded fresh fruit where the transaction is a "wholly intraprovincial" transaction. The Court affirmed that trading transactions occurring entirely within the provinces are an exclusive provincial jurisdiction (ss.92 [13], [16] BNA Act) and decided, in narrow terms, that the federal grading program has no validity in relation to purely intraprovincial transactions and, in that respect, is *ultra vires*.

An interdepartmental task force was convened to consider the ramifications of these judgements and to present options to cabinet with regard to federal and provincial grades and standards prescription and implementation. The current state (in the most general terms) as a result of these decisions is that the federal government has jurisdiction over grades and standards of food products moving interprovincially, while the provinces can prevent the sale of food products that do not meet provincial standards (including those in compliance with Food and Drug Regulations). If a province has no grades or standards (as in most cases), then the Food and Drugs standards are not valid, whereas CAPS Act standards, which apply only to interprovincial and international trade, would be valid. These cases provide a potential for fragmentation of standards across Canada that would create tremendous barriers to movement of food and agricultural products interprovincially.

The following are examples of barriers created through grades and standards manipulation and inspection practices:

- Quebec, the Maritime provinces and the federal government all define a Number 1 Grade table potato as being 2.25 to 3.5 inches, while Ontario Number 1 table potato has a minimum size of 2 inches. Quebec officials argued that this gave Ontario a cost advantage, for although the potatoes were marked "Ontario Number 1" and not "Canada Number 1," the consumer did not distinguish the two (in Quebec, producers graded their potatoes "Canada 1" rather than "Quebec 1" to gain a higher price). Prince Edward Island officials, however, felt that the smaller Ontario potato permitted the P.E.I. potato to be sold at a higher price as a more exclusive item and, therefore, did not perceive the grade discrepancy as a barrier.

- Quebec government officials stated that, depending on the supply situation in Ontario, the inspectors in Ontario would allow fruit and vegetables shipped by truck from Quebec to remain on the trucks long enough before inspection to go bad, thus ruining the Quebec producers' reputation at the retail level. Ontario industry representatives stated that the same sort of thing would happen in Manitoba when supplies from Ontario were not needed. Furthermore, the Manitoba Vegetable Producers Commission would rather trade with Texas than Ontario, which competed year-round. Generally, Ontario will not ship produce to Manitoba during the Manitoba growing season, but occasionally mixed loads will go, often to be rejected by Manitoba inspectors on the basis of quality.

- A comment was made by an Ontario official that grading for interprovincial movement is undertaken on the basis of the product *at that time,* and no consideration is made for ripening during shipment. On arrival and reinspection, the grade may have fallen, damaging the reputation of the shipper.

- An Ontario wholesaler expressed concern with the requirement

50

that produce be graded before interprovincial shipment. He stated that the market was such that the produce would be ordered at five o'clock in Quebec for sale in Ontario the next morning, and it was impossible to have a federal inspector grade the produce in the time available. Agriculture Canada is not strictly enforcing the regulation (by informal agreement), but it was the view of the wholesaler that should the regulation be enforced (and Agriculture Canada has the authority), it would make out-of-province fruit and vegetable purchases almost impossible.

- Concern was expressed by both Ontario retail industry officials and Quebec federal inspection officials with regard to the respective provinces "beefing up" of inspection forces: in Ontario for fruit and vegetable inspection at retail (due to the *Dominion* case), and in Quebec in the meat sector (due to the tainted-meat scandals). It was felt that these dramatic increases in the numbers of inspectors could potentially create interprovincial barriers in that there would be more overlapping of services, creating more room for uneven inspection practices.
- Quebec and Ontario, and Quebec and New Brunswick have agreed that "C" grade apples will not be traded interprovincially. Agriculture Canada, to help enforce the agreements, will not certify "C" grade apples for interprovincial shipment.
- Regional Consumer and Corporate Affairs officials in Quebec, responsible for enforcing provincial grades at retail (they cannot enforce the federal grades due to the *Labatt, Dominion* cases), stated that from time to time when produce in Quebec, such as tomatoes or apples, is in conflict with Ontario imports, the officials are "requested" to be more stringent in their inspections so as to stop the flow of produce from Ontario.
- In general terms, all federal grades, standards and inspections for the purpose of interprovincial trade are barriers to trade.
- Margarine-butter blends are permitted only in Saskatchewan and Nova Scotia. Legislation prohibits such blends in all other provinces, thus preventing trade interprovincially.

Although overlapping federal and provincial jurisdictions in the development and enforcement of grades and standards provide numerous opportunities to impede interprovincial trade, it would appear, with the exception of isolated incidents, that such regulations do not create major barriers to the free movement of food and agricultural products. However, the potential for a total fragmentation of standards across Canada exists with the recent Supreme Court decisions on *Labatt Breweries* and *Dominion Stores*. These decisions call into question the role of the federal government in the setting and enforcement of national (versus provincial) grades and standards. The effect of these decisions still remains to be seen.

Plant and Animal Health Regulation

The interprovincial movement of all agricultural commodities is subject to provincial and federal phyto-sanitary and animal health regulations. Such regulations are constantly changing, reflecting governmental attempts to localize newly discovered health problems or the disappearance of old health problems. It has been suggested that some of the regulations are merely an attempt to protect a provincial market from competition, but in order to substantiate such a claim, a technical analysis of the individual health risks would have to be undertaken. The following list merely sets forth examples of the types of health restrictions on the movement of various commodities:

- Pear trellis/rust: A British Columbia and federal government certification scheme requires juniper trees to be certified free from "rust" before sale of the trees (the obligatory alternate host) east of the Manitoba-Ontario border. The scheme has been implemented at the request of the B.C. Nursery Tree Association, since without the certification, British Columbia would not be able to sell the trees east of Manitoba or to the U.S. The association has suggested (unsubstantiated) that the disease is political (only B.C. has it) and that the rust that appears on pear tree leaves has no economic impact on the production or quality of the fruit
- Brucellosis: A disease that affects cattle. British Columbia and the Maritimes are currently free from the disease. When there is an outbreak, all movement from the affected area must cease.
- I.L.T. disease: British Columbia chickens have I.L.T. disease, while Alberta chickens are free of it. Therefore, Alberta can sell live chickens to B.C., but not vice versa (Alberta currently does not take advantage of this, since B.C. does not have adequate killing capacity).
- Petty infestation of ring rot: Seed potatoes in Alberta have petty infestation of ring rot while B.C. is free from this disease. As a consequence this product may not be shipped from Alberta to B.C.
- Newfoundland conducts a certification program for imported hogs. Currently, there is a disease-free hog herd on the island, which creates an excellent potential for national and international sales. Only certified disease-free hogs are permitted on the island.
- Health regulations and inspection requirements can create an in-

terprovincial barrier in that some regions can only support small food-processing plants, and such plants have difficulty covering the costs of compliance with such regulations. For example, P.E.I. was an exporter of poultry until the 1950s when small processing plants were forced to close because they could not meet the new health standards and remain competitive.

Health regulations may restrict movement even within provincial boundaries. For example, Saanich is a quarantine area for golden nematode (potatoes), and thus the potatoes may not be shipped from Vancouver Island. Golden nematode and potato wart also exist in Newfoundland, and exports are prohibited to prevent the spread of these pests.

The enforcement of plant and animal health regulations do obviously impede the free movement of agricultural products interprovincially. Such restraint is generally considered to be justified, although it was alleged (without substantiation) that health-related barriers were being used to protect local markets rather than to prevent the spread of a serious disease.

Summary and Conclusions 5

Summary

The following barriers to maintaining an integrated market for food and agricultural products have been identified:

- Transportation-related policies of the federal and provincial governments distort trade patterns or impede free movement of agricultural products. Federal transportation policies with a regional emphasis, such as Maritime and Atlantic region freight subsidies, Feed Freight Assistance, and statutory rates on the movement of Prairie grains to Thunder Bay (the Crow rate), have favoured, and still favour, the movement of raw agricultural products into Central Canada. These policies have, at the same time, hindered the development of livestock production and food processing in Western and Atlantic Canada.

  Trucking regulation is a provincial responsibility. Lack of uniformity of regulations between provinces complicates the interprovincial movement of goods by truck.

  Shortages of adequate transportation equipment are considered impediments to trade in two specific cases. Maritime potato farmers feel that movement of their product into markets in Central Canada is impeded by a shortage of refrigerated boxcars. Inadequate grain transportation facilities in the Prairie region are also considered an impediment to the interprovincial movement of feed grains.

- Agricultural marketing boards are associated with a number of different kinds of restriction to interprovincial trade. Licencing and other regulatory powers of marketing boards represent actual or potential control of product movement within and between provinces. The use of these controls has caused significant market distortions within Canada in the past and represents a major potential source of market distortions in the future.

Sharing the national market is central to the concept of national supply management marketing agencies such as those presently existing in the dairy and poultry sectors. While the provincial shares of the national market are technically negotiable, the nature of the federal-provincial agreements upon which they are based and the negotiation process by which market shares may be changed hinders relocation of production to regions where it can be accomplished most efficiently. The criteria by which changes in provincial market shares are negotiated intensify the problem, since they favour increased provincial self-sufficiency in production over optimal resource allocation.

Virtually all marketing boards prohibit interprovincial movement of products by individual producers. While this represents a barrier for producers as such, the actual restriction of trade in that commodity, or foods processed from it, will depend upon the control exercised by the marketing board at the primary and at other levels of the marketing chain. Outside the supply-managed commodities, most marketing boards have no control over interprovincial movement of the processed product. For example, in most provinces producers must market their *hogs* through provincial boards, but market distortion is considered minimal, since there are no barriers to the interprovincial movement of fresh *pork*.

- Government assistance with a regional or provincial emphasis may reduce the degree of integration of markets for agriculture and food products across Canada. The Department of Regional Economic Expansion is an example of a federal program that has the explicit objective of influencing production and trade patterns so as to achieve regional development goals. A further example is the substantial differences that exist between provincial agricultural policies, particularly in the areas of stabilization and credit, which are perceived to distort resource allocation.

The legitimacy of regional development objectives, whether pursued by federal or provincial governments, is generally recognized. The problem areas that are identified relate instead to inadequate evaluation of effects on other regions of federal or provincial programs in a specific region, the suspicion that some provincial programs are "predatory," and the feeling that single-minded pursuit of self-sufficiency rather than legitimate regional development is the real objective of many provincial programs.

- Provincial governments are substantial consumers of goods and services and as such are capable of influencing economic activity within the province by favouring local suppliers in their procurement activities. In many cases, this involves nothing more than choosing a local supplier over an out-of-province supplier— "everything else being equal." In other cases, local suppliers will be used even though their bids are higher than those of out-of-province suppliers. Other more subtle methods include evaluation of bids on the basis of "provincial value added," selective distribution of calls for tender, or inclusion of performance requirements that only local firms can meet.

- Provincial food and agricultural promotion programs, which exist in all provinces or regions to various extents, manifest the current provincial emphasis on self-sufficiency. Budgets vary from the modest annual expenditure of approximately $60,000 for the Saskatchewan's Own program, to several million dollars for Foodland Ontario. Promotional activity includes media campaigns, cost-sharing grants to commodity groups and marketing boards, and the use of moral suasion to encourage retailers to feature local produce under the appropriate logo. The impact of these programs is difficult to measure, but without a doubt they serve to increase the competitive advantage of the local product vis-à-vis "imported" products.

- The marketing and distribution of alcoholic beverages (particularly wines) represent a very clear and unapologetic barrier to the interprovincial movement of these products. The primary wine producing provinces of British Columbia, Ontario and Quebec provide the most striking examples of barriers, which virtually prohibit the sale of out-of-province Canadian wines. When possible, wineries are required to use local grapes exclusively. Liquor store policies with regard to listings (brands made available in liquor stores), distribution and markups favour local products over those imported from other provinces or countries. The barriers are not subtle and are clearly protectionist.

- Packaging and labelling regulations do not appear to create significant impediments to the movement of food and agricultural products, since the legislation is well standardized across Canada. There are, however, isolated examples such as inconsistencies regarding parchment and foil wrap for butter, and bottling legislation that restricts movement of soft drinks between provinces.

- Overlapping federal and provincial jurisdiction in the development and enforcement of grades and standards provides numerous opportunities to impede interprovincial trade. In the case of highly perishable produce, such as fresh fruit and vegetables, inspection procedures have allegedly been used to discourage movement. For instance, accusations have been made that inspectors in Ontario and Manitoba have on occasion unduly delayed inspection of produce arriving from out of province, thereby causing its deterioration and, consequently, reducing the competitiveness of out-of-province produce.

Two recent court cases, *Labatt Breweries* v. *The Queen* and *Dominion Stores* v. *The Queen*, have brought into question the role of the federal government in setting and enforcing national (versus provincial) grades and standards. Without a clarification of this issue, there is a danger that a proliferation of non-uniform provincial standards will result in a fragmentation of standards across Canada, creating potential barriers to the movement of food and agricultural products interprovincially.

- Plant and animal health regulation can be a potential source of trade impediment. Prevention of product movement for health reasons is usually seen as being justified. Restricted movement of live hogs into Newfoundland, for instance, is necessary to preserve the specific pathogen-free status of the swine population there. In a few cases, however, it is alleged that health-related barriers are being used to protect local markets rather than to prevent the spread of serious disease.

Conclusions

Impediments to interprovincial trade in food and agricultural products do exist in Canada. Just as important, other conditions necessary for the maintenance of a highly integrated market have been violated or are in danger of being violated. This is not surprising, since distortions of trade flows and resource allocation are the by-product or even the intent of regulatory policies and programs of both the federal and provincial governments.

Any lack of uniformity in government policies will have an impact on resource allocation by creating artificial advantage or disadvantage in one region compared to others. This is particularly true within a confederation where there is a division of powers between the two levels of government and independence in specified policy areas.

In this study, several factors that impede interprovincial trade flows and distort the allocation of resources within the national economy have been identified. Some have a substantial economic impact, whereas others have a less significant effect but are, nevertheless, irritating to those involved in particular markets.

Plant and animal health regulations, and packaging and labelling standards occasionally create product movement and market differentiation problems for the food-processing and distribution sectors. Anecdotes about the deleterious consequences of such regulation abound, but in general, these are considered to have relatively minor economic consequences.

The use of provincial grades and standards to impede interprovincial trade in agricultural and food products has not been a major issue in Canada. However, recent Supreme Court decisions that bring into question the validity of federal grades and standards in relation to purely *intra*provincial transactions could lead to a fragmentation of standards along provincial lines that could, in turn, lead to the creation of significant barriers to the movement of food products between provinces.

Provincial liquor control regulations are a prime example of the extent to which interprovincial trade can be constrained within the present legislative framework, which gives provincial governments rather wide discretionary powers over the sale of beer, wines and spirits. Surprisingly, this overt violation of the principle of free trade between the provinces does not cause widespread concern. To a large extent, this reflects a tacit agreement between the provincial government, grape growers, and the wineries to focus their merchandising efforts within the province rather than compete in a national market. As such, a *de facto* market-sharing agreement for wine products can be considered to exist in Canada.

A growing emphasis on provincial self-sufficiency is manifested in food promotional programs and the procurement policies of provincial governments. At the same time there is a growing disparity between provinces with regard to provincially funded subsidies at all levels of the food system, and also with regard to the stabilization of markets for raw agricultural products. These provincial programs have an important impact on trade flows and the location of production. They create "discrimination" between markets by distinguishing between products of provincial origin and others. They influence the allocation of resources and the location of production by creating artificial advantages for local producers over those in other provinces.

The most important factors reducing the degree of integration in Canadian agricultural and food markets are, paradoxically, the result of federal rather than provincial policy initiatives. The programs that are the manifestation of such policies are of two major types:

- transportation subsidies, such as the statutory Crow's Nest Pass freight rates, Feed Freight Assistance, and the Atlantic region freight rates;
- market-sharing arrangements under the federal-provincial agreements with regard to broiler chickens, eggs, turkeys and industrial milk.

Transportation policies, and in particular those relating to the subsidized movement of grain, have caused serious distortions in the allocation of resources across the nation. Specifically, subsidized transportation of grain has given economic advantages to grain producers in Western Canada and livestock producers in Eastern Canada and British Columbia, and placed livestock producers in Western Canada and grain producers outside the Prairie region at a relative disadvantage. The regional pattern of growth and development in the livestock-slaughtering and meat-processing industry in Canada has also been distorted as a result of these programs. Both the Crow rate and Feed Freight Assistance were initially established for sound reasons. Yet, over time they became institutionalized, and successive governments, largely for reasons of political expediency, have shied away from making the necessary changes to reassert the integrity of the common market for products and to maintain an efficient distribution of productive resources within the national economy.

Market-sharing agreements are a relatively new phenomenon in Canadian agriculture. They are nevertheless somewhat of an anachronism in a nation that has an avowed commitment to a high degree of economic integration. Worse still, it is apparent that at senior levels of government there is a desire to extend supply management and market-sharing agreements to other agricultural commodities. From a short-term perspective, such programs have much to recommend them to government, for they entail no significant government expenditure or involvement in market management. However, they result in the balkanization and subsequent ossification of the location of production, they take little or no account of changes in regional comparative advantage, and they represent a policy focus that is the very antithesis of a common market for agricultural and food products within Canada.

The appropriate handling of these issues in the Constitution is a complex problem, given the need to preserve provincial autonomy in certain policy areas:

> Both the provincial and federal governments can erode the economic union and diminish the gains from it by the exercise of some of their regulatory and spending powers. We must consider how far harmonization in these other functions requires constitutional expression rather than simply continuing co-operation at the policy level.[1]

It is apparent from interpretation of relevant sections of the BNA Act in various court cases that there is no constitutional guarantee of

---

[1] A.E. Safarian, *Canadian Federalism and Economic Integration* (Ottawa: Information Canada, 1974), p. 5.

free movement of goods interprovincially, only that no tariffs shall be charged at interprovincial boundaries. More recently, an increasingly adversarial rather than cooperative attitude among the provinces and between the provinces and the federal government is apparent in policy formulation. When federal government commitment to policies that encourage market segmentation rather than consolidation (of which national marketing agencies are perhaps the best example) is added to this list of considerations, it is clear that the prospects for preservation of a high degree of economic integration in the agriculture and food sector is indeed bleak without constitutional constraints on both levels of government. The stakes are not only economic. Failure to preserve a high degree of economic integration will not only adversely affect the economic welfare of Canadians but will also almost certainly reduce the desirability of political union.

Interprovincial Barriers to Trade: Constitutional Context

Canada's constitutional review has focussed, in large part, on the maintenance of an "economic union" in this country, defined as an "area within which goods and services can be bought and sold between its various parts without being subject to customs duties or other barriers, and within which there are no legal or fiscal barriers to the movement of people or capital."[1] This economic union was a vital component of the social contract agreed to in 1867 and is explicitly recognized in section 121 of the British North America Act, which states, "All Articles of the Growth, Produce, or Manufacture of any one of the Provinces shall, from and after the Union, be admitted free into each of the other Provinces." However, court interpretation has clearly indicated that while section 121 prohibits the imposition of custom duties on the movement of goods between provinces, it does not preclude non-fiscal impediments to the movement of goods, nor does it prohibit the imposition of other kinds of taxes that might impede the free flow of goods. Duff, J. in *Gold Seal Ltd. v. A.G. of Alberta*[2] limited the scope of section 121 by stating that the "...real object of the clause is to prohibit the establishment of customs duties affecting interprovincial trade in the products of any province of the Union." Crocket, J. in *Atlantic Smoke Shops Ltd. v. Conlon*[3] referred to the *Gold Seal* case as follows:

> Whether or not the decision means that the section (121) only applies to Dominion legislation it plainly implies ... that the parliament of Canada may validly go as far as to expressly prohibit the admission from one province to another of any article of growth, produce or manufacture of

---

[1] Document 830-81/006, Meeting of the Continuing Committee of Ministers on the Constitution, 8-11 July 1980.

[2] (1921) 62 S.C.R. 424, 62 D.L.R. 62.

[3] (1941) S.C.R. 670, (1941) 4 D.L.R. 129.

another province so long as the prohibition does not involve the imposition of a custom duty.

A series of Supreme Court of Canada and Privy Council decisions following the *Gold Seal* case has reiterated Duff, J.'s interpretation of section 121, although there have been dissenting opinions, most significantly that of Rand, J. in *Murphy* v. *C.P.R. & A.G. Canada*[4] wherein he states that section 121 was directed " . . . against trade regulation which is designed to place fetters on or raise impediments to or otherwise restrict or limit the free flow of commerce across the Dominion as if provincial boundaries did not exist."[5] It must be considered, however, at this time, that section 121 is to be narrowly interpreted as directed at the formation of a customs union and not a common market.[6] Thus, there is no constitutional guarantee of free movement of goods interprovincially.

Another provision of the BNA Act relevant to the free movement of goods interprovincially is section 91 (2), which gives Parliament the exclusive legislative jurisdiction over "The Regulation of Trade and Commerce." The courts have interpreted this section as embracing only interprovincial and international trade, and as meaning, in general, that provincial trade regulations that create direct barriers to the interprovincial movement of goods are *ultra vires*. For example, in the *Manitoba Egg Reference*[7] the Supreme Court of Canada struck down the provincial marketing board scheme that effectively imposed a quota on the importation of eggs produced out of province. British Columbia unsuccessfully attempted also to restrict the importation of eggs by requiring that each egg imported into the province bear the name of its country of origin in ink. The Court held that the indirect effect of the legislation was to make it impossible to import eggs into B.C., and thus the legislation was declared invalid.[8]

The provinces have jurisdiction over property and civil rights in the province (section 92 [13], BNA Act), and through this power they may regulate intraprovincial trade. The provinces have a great capacity to create interprovincial barriers (for example, provincial product stan-

---

[4] (1958) S.C.R. 626, 15 D.L.R. (2d) 145.

[5] Ibid., p. 642.

[6] It is interesting to note that although the federal government has been advocating the inclusion of a clause in section 121 to prevent the imposition of barriers to the free movement of goods *(inter alia)*, in their recent repatriation proposal this amendment was not included.

[7] *A.G. Manitoba* v. *Manitoba Egg and Poultry Association* (1971) S.C.R. 689.

[8] *Crickard et al.* v. *A.G. British Columbia* (1958) 25 W.W.R. 485.

dards legislation, in the light of Labatt's "Special Lite" case. could potentially cripple the flow of standard goods interprovincially). Provincial procurement policies, packaging, labelling, health and safety legislation all find their constitutional basis in the power given through section 92 (13).

Marketing boards, whether solely provincial or as part of a national scheme, provide a fertile area for the study of market distortions and interprovincial barriers peculiar to food and agriculture. It is only through a joint exercise of federal and provincial powers that marketing boards may exercise interprovincial trade powers (the concurrent federal/provincial jurisdiction in relation to agriculture in section 95 has been interpreted narrowly to encompass the production but not regulation of trade of natural products).

Marketing board legislation passed through several phases before attaining its current form, acceptable under the Constitution. The federal Natural Products Marketing Act passed in 1934 lasted only two and one-half years before being declared *ultra vires* on the grounds of its infringing upon the provincial property and civil rights jurisdiction. Following this decision, provincial boards were created with, ostensibly, solely intraprovincial spheres of influence. A series of Supreme Court and Privy Council decisions upheld the provincial schemes, provided they were in essence "intraprovincial." In *Shannon* v. *Lower Mainland Dairy Products Board*,[9] the provincial scheme for the compulsory marketing of milk through the provincial board, including milk produced in other provinces, was upheld as a legal scheme, in that its application to milk produced out of province was merely an "incident of an essentially intraprovincial scheme." This case and others suggested that the courts would accept a very extensive power to regulate marketing within the province, notwithstanding the incidental effects on other provinces.

In 1945, by the Agricultural Products Marketing Act, the federal Parliament gave power to the Governer General in Council (that is, the federal cabinet) to delegate to provincial marketing boards the power to regulate the marketing of agricultural products "outside the province in interprovincial and export trade." Section 2 of the act reads as follows:

> 2(1) The Governor in Council may by order grant authority to any board or agency authorized under the law of any province to exercise powers of regulation in relation to the marketing of any agricultural product locally within the province, to regulate the marketing of such agricultural product outside the province in interprovincial and export trade and for such

---

[9] (1938) A.C. 708.

purposes to exercise all or any powers like the powers exercisable by such board or agency in relation to the marketing of such agricultural product locally within the province.

(2) The Governor in Council may by order revoke any authority granted under subsection one.

On the face of it, this delegation of power did not appear to be legal. The decision in the *Nova Scotia Inter-Delegation*[10] case (1950) denied to the various Canadian legislative bodies the power to delegate their powers to each other. This creates a great deal of inflexibility in constitutional adaptation, and the courts have, since that case, found ways to subvert its meaning. The Agricultural Products Marketing Act was tested in P.E.I.: in *Potato Marketing Board* v. *Willis*[11] the province established a provincial potato marketing board, and the federal government, acting under the authority of the federal statute, then delegated to the P.E.I. Potato Marketing Board interprovincial and export trade powers with regard to the marketing of potatoes. The Supreme Court of Canada held that this was a legal delegation of powers, since they flowed not to a provincial legislature but to an administrative agency created by the provincial legislature. Thus administrative interdelegation was a valid exercise, while legislative interdelegation was not.[12]

Provincial agricultural surpluses in conjunction with interprovincial marketing board powers created chaos in the late 1960s and early 1970s (the notorious chicken and egg war), and prompted the formation of national marketing boards for commodities that the producers and provinces felt should be so regulated. The Farm Products Marketing Agencies Act[13] provided for the establishment of national marketing agencies where the "majority of the producers of the farm product or products concerned are in favour of such an agency."

A.E. Safarian summarizes the current state of law with regard to agricultural marketing legislation as follows:

(1) The federal government normally has not the authority to regulate the intraprovincial movement of products, but provinces have such authority.
(2) Provinces have not the authority to regulate the interprovincial movement of products, but the federal government can extend interprovincial powers to provincial boards.

---

[10] *A.G.N.S.* v. *A.G. Canada* (1951) S.C.R. 31, (1950) 4 D.L.R. 369.

[11] (1952) 2 S.C.R. 392, (1952) 4 D.L.R. 146.

[12] P.W. Hogg, *Constitutional Law of Canada* (Toronto: The Carswell Company of Canada, 1977).

[13] S.C. 1970-71-72, c. 65.

(3) Provinces can charge license fees under a marketing scheme to defray costs of regulating a product and to increase the general funds of the province (direct taxation), but cannot charge a levy for price adjustment purposes (indirect taxation).

(4) A system of pooling of returns under a provincial marketing scheme was held to be valid.

(5) The regulation of a product delivered within a province was considered to be within the competence of provincial legislation even though, after processing, most of the by-products moved into interprovincial trade.[14]

A further influence in the creation of national marketing plans was (and is) Canada's membership in GATT (General Agreement on Tariffs and Trade), an international trading system that lays down agreed rules for international trade. The fundamental principles and aims of the agreement are the reduction of tariffs and other barriers to trade and the elimination of discriminatory treatment in international commerce. In order to comply with GATT in limitation of imports of agricultural commodities, Canada must have an effective domestic supply management program. This has been interpreted as national supply management programs by advocates of such plans.

Other interprovincial barriers to trade identified in this study, such as differential subsidies, have no constitutional limitations but are subject only to the practical limits imposed by provincial or national treasuries. Thus, there is little in the Constitution to prevent the use of subsidies, direct or indirect, that affect the interests of out-of-province producers.

---

[14] A.E. Safarian, *Canadian Federalism and Economic Integration* (Ottawa: Privy Council Office, 1974), p. 50.

Provincial Stabilization Programs

The following summaries of provincial stabilization programs are based on material obtained from Agriculture Canada in July 1980.

1. **British Columbia Farm Income Assurance Program**
   Objective: To ensure farmers an economic status comparable to that of other skilled groups in society.

   Program Outline: Five-year stabilization plans were established for over twenty commodities. All plans have terminated, and new agreements are being negotiated between producers and the province. The basic pattern for the new agreements involves support payments when the average annual price is less than 100 per cent of the estimated total cost of production (excluding returns to land and management). Program costs are shared between producers and the province on a 50:50 basis.

   Target Clients: All farm operators who produce and sell hogs, strawberries for processing, peas, beans and corn, cherries, apricots, peaches, plums, prunes, pears and apples.

   Eligibility Criteria: Producers who are in "good standing" with the relevant commodity organization designated by the British Columbia Federation of Agriculture, who pay premiums into the appropriate commodity stabilization fund, and who have an enterprise of a size at least equal to the minimum established for that type of production. A maximum eligibility is established for each type of enterprise.

2. **Alberta Hog Stabilization Program**
   Objective: To restore confidence and prevent erosion of the industry through the negative impact of low producer prices and increased production costs.

Program Outline: Producers are guaranteed $35 over feed costs for a standard hog (170 lbs., index 101). Support payments equal to the difference between the support price (adjusted monthly for changes in feed costs) and the weekly average market price are made monthly. Program costs are totally borne by the province.

Target Clients: All hog producers.

Eligibility Criteria: All marketed hogs originating from the province of Alberta.

Note: Program announced 12 May 1980 is effective 1 April 1980 until 31 March 1981.

3. **Saskatchewan Hog Assured Returns Program**
   Objective: To provide income security to hog producers.

   Program Outline: Hog prices are stabilized on a quarterly basis through a 50:50 cost-sharing agreement between producers and the province. Support payments are made when the quarterly average price received by participating producers is less than cash costs of production plus 85 per cent of non-cash costs.

   Target Clients: All hog producers.

   Eligibility Criteria: Marketing of hogs through Saskatchewan Hog Marketing Commission and payment of premiums to the stabilization fund. Maximum eligibility: 1,000 hogs for individual producers; 3,000 hogs for partnerships and corporations.

4. **Manitoba Beef Producer Income Assurance Plan**
   Objective: To encourage producers to shift from cow-calf to slaughter beef production.

   Program Outline: The program provides annual support payments for feeder calves and slaughter cattle when the average market price is less than a support price equal to the estimated cash cost of production plus depreciation, replacement cost of cull cows, labour costs and 50 per cent of interest on investment. When the market price is above the support price, producers pay the difference to the government as a refund, but the maximum refund paid by the producer cannot exceed the amount he received from the program. Producers agree to fatten a progressively larger share of their calves to slaughter weight.

   Target Clients: All cow-calf producers.

Eligibility Criteria: All persons with beef cows who enroll in the program. Maximum eligibility: 70 cows.

5. **Ontario Beef Cow-Calf Stabilization Program**
Objective: To stabilize the income of producers.

Program Outline: Annual support payments for feeder calves are made when the average market price is less than the estimated cash costs of production plus depreciation, plus 70 per cent of the interest on investment and the return to operator labour and management. Program costs are intended to be shared between producers and the province on a 1/3:2/3 basis.

Target Clients: All beef cow-calf producers in the province.

Eligibility Criteria: All beef cow-calf producers in the province who sell feeder calves and pay program enrollment fees.

6. **Ontario Farm Income Stabilization Program**
Objective: To stabilize the income of producers.

Program Outline: Annual support payments are made when the average market price is less than 95 per cent of the five-year average price plus an adjustment for changes in cash costs of production. However, if a support payment is made under the federal program, the provincial support payment only makes up the difference between the federal and provincial support prices. Prices are stabilized through a cost-sharing agreement between producers and the province on a 1/3:2/3 basis.

Target Clients: All farm operators who produce and sell winter wheat, corn, soybeans and white beans.

Eligibility Criteria: All farm operators whose ordinary residence is in Ontario, who pay premiums into the commodity stabilization fund, and who have an enterprise at least equal to the minimum established for that type of production. A maximum eligibility is established for each type of enterprise.

7. **Quebec Farm Income Assurance Program**
Objective: To protect the efficient family-type farm by guaranteeing farm operators a positive net annual income.

Program Outline: Support payments are made when cash income is less than the estimated cost of production, including a return for the producer's labour (valued at a percentage of a skilled worker's annual wage, this percentage varies among commodities). Program costs are shared between producers and the province on a 1/3:2/3 basis.

Target Clients: All farm operators who produce and sell weanling pigs, feeder calves, slaughter cattle, potatoes, corn, wheat, oats, barley and mixed grains.

Eligibility Criteria: Farm operators who agree to pay annual premiums into the commodity fund for a five-year period, and who have an enterprise of a size at least equal to the minimum established for that type of production. A maximum eligibility is established for each type of enterprise.

8. P.E.I. Hog Price Stabilization Plan
Objective: To stabilize hog production and returns through a stop-loss policy of guaranteed minimum returns, not intended as an incentive.

Program Outline: Grants to producers enrolled in the program, covering half of the difference between base and market prices when cost of production exceeds market returns. Base price adjusted quarterly.

Target Clients: P.E.I. hog producers.

9. Nova Scotia Hog Stabilization Plan
Objective: To instill greater security, stability and confidence in the hog industry by assuring producers and processors of greater consistency in market returns and supply.

Program Outline: Producer assistance in the form of differential payments covering the margin created when costs of production exceed market price. The stabilization fund is maintained by both government and producer contributions.

Target Clients: Hog producers marketing through the Nova Scotia Hog Marketing Board.

10. New Brunswick Hog Price Stabilization Plan
Objective: To instill stability and security in the hog industry through a stop-loss policy.

Program Outline: Compensation to producers when the market price of hogs falls below the established base price. Payouts are shared equally by the fund and government. Producer contribution to the fund is required when market price exceeds the base price by $5.00/cwt.

Target Clients: Bona fide hog producers marketing through the N.B. Hog Marketing Board.

Bibliography

Agriculture Canada. *Orientation of Canadian Agriculture: Domestic Policies and External Factors Which Have Influenced the Development of Canadian Agriculture.* Ottawa: 1977.

Agriculture Canada. *Policies and Programs for Agriculture: Atlantic Provinces.* Ottawa: 1978.

Agriculture Canada. *Policies and Programs for Agriculture: Federal.* Ottawa: 1976.

Agriculture Canada. *Policies and Programs for Agriculture: Ontario and Quebec.* Ottawa: 1979.

Agriculture Canada. *Policies and Programs for Agriculture: Western Provinces.* Ottawa: 1979.

Arcus, Peter L. "The Impact of Changes in the Statutory Freight Rates for Grain." In *Freight Rates and the Marketing of Canadian Agricultural Products.* Winnipeg: Department of Agricultural Economics and Farm Management, University of Manitoba, August 1977.

Atlantic Provinces Economic Council. *Atlantic Canada Today.* Halifax: 1977.

Broadwith, Hughes & Associates Ltd. "The Ontario Milk Marketing Board: An Economic Analysis." In *Government Regulation.* Ontario Economic Council, 1978.

Canada Grains Council. *Domestic Feed Grain Policy Study: A Report of the Advisory Committee.* Winnipeg: Canada Grains Council, October 1979.

Canada Grains Council. *Key Issues in Canadian Grain Transportation: A Background Paper.* Winnipeg: n.d.

Department of Regional Economic Expansion. *Annual Report 1978-79.* Ottawa: 1980.

Drummond, W.M.; Anderson, W.J.; and Kerr, T.C. *A Review of Agricultural Policy in Canada.* Ottawa: Agricultural Economics Research Council of Canada, 1966.

Foodwest Resource Consultants. *Pork Industry in the Alberta Economy.* Edmonton: March 1980.

Hogg, Peter W. *Constitutional Law of Canada.* Toronto: The Carswell Company, 1977.

Laskin, Bora. *Laskin's Canadian Constitutional Law.* 4th rev. ed. Edited by Albert S. Abel. Toronto: The Carswell Company, 1975.

Maritime Union Study. *The Report on Maritime Union.* Halifax: 1970.

McCarten, W.J. "The Atlantic Provinces' Stake in the Canadian Economic Union." Paper prepared for the conference, The Atlantic Provinces in Canada: Social Science Perspectives, University of Moncton, May 1980.

Office of the Privy Council. *Commission on the Costs of Transporting Grain by Rail: Report.* Vol. 1. Ottawa: Department of Supply and Services, October 1976.

Safarian, A.E. *Canadian Federalism & Economic Integration.* Ottawa: Privy Council Office, 1974.

Safarian, A.E. *Ten Markets or One? Regional Barriers to Economic Activity in Canada.* Toronto: Ontario Economic Council (Discussion Paper Series), 1980.

Saskatchewan Agriculture. "A Look at Canada's Domestic Feed Grains Policy." In *Farm Notes*, vol. 6, no. 3, April 1980.

Saskatchewan Natural Products Marketing Council. *The Domestic Feed Grain Market Performance: 1976 to 1979.* Regina: 1979.

Select Standing Committee on Agriculture, Legislative Assembly, British Columbia. *The Impact of the Department of Regional Economic Expansion on the Food Industry in Western Canada.* May 1978.

Select Standing Committee on Agriculture, Legislative Assembly, British Columbia. *Tariff and Non-tariff Barriers Affecting the Food Industry in British Columbia.* August 1978.

Whyte, J.D., and Lederman, W.R. *Canadian Constitutional Law.* 2nd ed. Toronto: Butterworths, 1977.

The Canadian Institute for Economic Policy Series

The Monetarist Counter-Revolution: A Critique of Canadian Monetary Policy 1975-1979
Arthur W. Donner and Douglas D. Peters

Canada's Crippled Dollar: An Analysis of International Trade and Our Troubled Balance of Payments.
H. Lukin Robinson

Unemployment and Inflation: The Canadian Experience
Clarence L. Barber and John C. P. McCallum

How Ottawa Decides: Planning and Industrial Policy-Making 1968-1980
Richard D. French

Energy and Industry: The Potential of Energy Development Projects for Canadian Industry in the Eighties
Barry Beale

The Energy Squeeze: Canadian Policies for Survival
Bruce F. Willson

The Post-Keynesian Debate: A Practical Guide to Current Economic Policy Trends in Canada
Myron J. Gordon

Water: The Emerging Crisis in Canada
Harold D. Foster and W. R. Derrick Sewell

The Working Poor: Wage Earners and the Failure of Income Security Policies
David P. Ross

After the Monetarists: Post-Keynesian Alternatives to Rampant Inflation, Low Growth and High Unemployment
Edited by David Crane

The above titles are available from:

James Lorimer & Company, Publishers
Egerton Ryerson Memorial Building
35 Britain Street
Toronto M5A 1R7, Ontario

DATE DUE

"That Man Partridge"

E.A. Partridge, His Thoughts and Times

Murray Knuttila

Canadian Plains Research Center
University of Regina
1994

Copyright @ Canadian Plains Research Center

Canadian Plains Research Center
University of Regina
Regina, Saskatchewan S4S 0A2
Canada

Canadian Cataloguing in Publication Data
Knuttila, Kenneth Murray
    "That man Partridge"

(Canadian plains studies, ISSN 0317-6290 ; 26)
ISBN 0-88977-079-4

1. Partridge, Edward Alexander, d. 1931.
2. Agriculturists – Prairie Provinces – Biography.
3. Businessmen – Prairie Provinces – Political
activities. 4. Grain trade – Prairie Provinces –
History. I. University of Regina. Canadian Plains
Research Center. II. Title. III. Series.

HD1786.5.P37K58 1994   338.1'092   C94-920194-4

Cover Design: Agnes Bray/Brian Mlazgar
Cover photograph reproduced courtesy of the Saskatchewan Wheat Pool
(photograph R-B 7778, Saskatchewan Archives Board-Regina)
Printed and bound in Canada by
Hignell Printing Limited, Winnipeg, Manitoba
Printed on acid-free paper

For the thousands who built this province, including Liisa and Gabriel Knuttila, Mary and George Kubik, Jenny and Aaron Salo, and in the memory of Edwin Knuttila.

Contents

Acknowledgments

A great many people assisted my research over the years, including the staff at the Saskatchewan Archives Board-Regina, the National Archives, Queen's University Archives, the Archives of the United Grain Growers, and descendants of E.A. Partridge. Financial support was provided by SSHRC through the President's General Research Grant Fund at the University of Regina. I thank Wendee Kubik for her support and helpful commentary. The manuscript was improved thanks to the comments of anonymous reviewers. The project would not have been possible without the continued support of James N. McCrorie and the staff at CPRC. The editorial work of Brian Mlazgar and Agnes Bray deserves special thanks and acknowledgment.

Introduction

Human beings have demonstrated a propensity to ask simple, yet profound, questions about themselves. Examples of such questions are: how can we understand human behaviour? what factors explain our attitudes, emotions, character and personality? or even, why do humans, as a species, exhibit such a range of different behaviours, attitudes, actions and outlooks?

For as long as humans have asked these questions, they have been attempting to provide answers for them. The answers that have been developed offer radically different explanations, explanations that range from the arguments of biological determinists, who maintain that most human behaviours and characteristics are genetically or biologically determined, to those that rely on religious doctrines and claims regarding the true "nature" of humans. As popular as some of these explanations may be in the public eye or the media, many social scientists tend to be skeptical when it comes to simplistic and reductionist arguments that seek to attribute complex human actions and characteristics to simple factors.

There is a rich tradition of thought in social science disciplines such as anthropology, sociology and social psychology which maintains that we can only understand human individuals by connecting them to their social surroundings and experiences. One of the most eloquent presentations of this argument is found in the work of the late C.W. Mills in his important book, *The Sociological Imagination*. The title is actually much more complicated than the essential argument he develops. According to Mills, every individual possesses a unique life story; however he argues that in order to make sense of an individual's life, we must locate him or her in the context of the larger historical and social environment in which he or she developed and lived. Mills maintains that it is both the promise and the task of the social sciences to improve our capacity to understand human beings by developing our ability to connect the lives and life stories of people to their social and historical contexts. Though other social scientists might use jargon like "connecting agency with structure" in referring to what Mills is saying, we should keep in mind that, if we want to improve our capacity to understand our lives and those of others, all we need to do is to place those lives in their larger social and historical setting.

In what follows we will attempt to understand the life and times of E.A. (Edward Alexander) Partridge in the manner suggested by Mills. The reader will meet Partridge and be encouraged to try to make sense of his life, who he was, what he became, how he acted, and what he

1

thought, by placing him in the context of his society and the historical period in which he lived. In what follows an effort will be made to use what we know about the life of Partridge in order to better understand the processes through which human individuals are on the one hand moulded and fashioned by history and society while they mould and shape history and society themselves.

E.A. Partridge is an excellent case study of how the individual, society and history are intimately bound together. His was a fascinating, at times unbelievable, and at other times mundane story. In a very real sense, Partridge represents all of the joys, ironies, contradictions, victories, defeats, tragedies and pleasures that comprise human life. Partridge was both an ordinary and extraordinary person whose story, when placed in the context of his times, offers insights into the forces that mould us and why generations of people have struggled to improve the lot of humankind.

This short volume had its origin in a project that started out as a biography of Partridge. The study of western Canadian history reveals the importance of E.A. Partridge. He was present when the Territorial Grain Growers' Association was founded. He was the founder of the Grain Growers' Grain Company, which eventually developed into the United Grain Growers. An activist in the Saskatchewan Grain Growers' Association, he was made an honourary president of the first farmers' union. He was present and participated in the political process that resulted in the formation of the Progressive Party, and advocated a "cooperative commonwealth" as early as 1905. He proposed the formation of an independent nation in the West, tried to set up a second grain company, was present for the debates over the wheat pools, and was part of an effort to establish a western bank. Equally astonishing is the fact that no adequate published accounts of his life exist. The standard reference is Ralph Hedlin's short work, which does not do Partridge justice. The present work will attempt to rectify this situation.

The lack of a published biography documenting the life of Partridge is easily explained — the data necessary to produce such a work do not exist. No personal papers or diaries survive, nor do any lengthy accounts by contemporaries seem to exist. Apparently, several rich sources did exist in various forms but these met with tragic ends before being digested by anyone interested in reconstructing and understanding Partridge's life.

The absence of such information and data rule out the possibility of preparing a standard biography; however since we do have access to substantial information on the society and social processes of which Partridge was a part, we can make an effort to understand his life and times. What follows is a reconstruction of aspects of that society and its processes, with as much consideration as possible of the role played by Partridge.

2

Perhaps the best way of introducing the reader to what follows is to first point out what we were and were not able to do. We were not able to present details of Partridge's personal life. We were not able to reconstruct the precise features of his personality, the influences which were formative in his philosophy and thinking, or present an adequate account of the social, political and intellectual forces which influenced his rich and provocative thought. On the other hand, we were able to attempt to provide some information about his life, the social processes of which he was a part and certain elements of his thought. We were able to attempt to show how he was shaped by, and in turn shaped, the environment in which he lived. Indeed this latter task is the central focus of this work. Let us therefore get on with the task of examining Partridge in an effort to understand the relationship between, and the intersection of, society and the individual by first examining the larger historical processes that brought Partridge to the West.

We begin with a discussion of the larger historical context within which western Canadian society developed. Chapter 1 presents an overview of the emergence of the National Policy and how the government policies associated with it influenced western development and those, such as Partridge, who were part of this grand historical process. This chapter also discusses how and why the National Policy produced the important social phenomenon that has come to be known as the western Canadian agrarian movement. Chapter 2 provides an overview of Partridge's role in the emerging protest movement with emphasis on the efforts of the organized farmers to address what they saw as the weaknesses in the grain-handling system. Chapter 3 outlines the struggles of farmers for tariff reform, and how their persistent failures served to radicalize some farmers and lead them to question the very structures of the political system. In this chapter we learn of E.A. and Mary Partridge's personal traumas and how these processes served to radicalize his thinking. Late in his life Partridge published a book, *A War on Poverty*, in which he systematically presents a critique of his society and his vision of a future social world. Chapter 4 discusses some of his ideas as presented in the book, using as much as possible his own words to convey his thoughts and ideas. The final chapter attempts to draw out the key lessons that can be gleaned from the life and times of E.A. Partridge, lessons that speak to how humans are both producers and products of their society and historical epochs. Paul Baran's concept of an intellectual is used to understand the development of E.A. Partridge and his role in Canadian society.

CHAPTER 1

The Historical Context: Confederation and the West

Industrialization, Nation Building, and the West

E.A. Partridge travelled to the Prairies and took up a homestead in the 1880s. He was part of a grand scheme of nation building that was undertaken after the creation of Canada in 1867. The formal creation of Canada was but one aspect of a larger set of economic and political developments that were occurring during the post-1867 period. Indeed, we now know that Confederation was only the first in a series of steps which were to be undertaken in order to facilitate the development of an industrial capitalist economy in Canada.

The use of the word "facilitate" here is deliberate because one of the fascinating aspects of Canadian history and development has been the central role played by the state. Indeed, Confederation itself, the creation of a new state, was the essential first step in providing a framework for the emergence of a new society. That the creation of a new state was but the first step in a larger economic and social development strategy is obvious if we examine the debates which occurred in the Canadian House of Commons as the proposal was first considered (Waite, 1963). Vernon Fowke (1957: 8) suggests that it is appropriate to call the general economic development policies that unfolded prior to and after Confederation the National Policy:

> the term national policy, without capitals, comprises collectively that group of policies and instruments which were designed to transform the British North American territories of the mid-nineteenth century into a political and economic unit.

What eventually emerged in the post-Confederation period were a number of specific and interconnected federal policies, including the construction of a transcontinental railway, the establishment of protective tariffs to promote and foster Canadian industry, and the provision of a domestic market for Canadian industry by settling the West with a population of agricultural producers. The creation of an agricultural population in the West was a central aspect of this plan because this population was to play a dual role in the National Policy. First, it was to produce cash crops for export, an activity that would benefit export merchants, transportation interests and food processors. Second, prairie farmers would have to buy numerous different types of industrial and manufactured goods in order to establish their farms and undertake the

4

production of cash crops — manufactured goods which central Canadian industrialists would supply.

Canadian academics have debated the precise nature of the development which was envisioned, and which economic and political interests advocated which policies; however, it is generally agreed that at the time of Confederation the major capitalist activity in Canada was confined to commercial and mercantile activities (Fowke, 1957; Naylor, 1975; Pentland, 1981; Ryerson, 1968). Clearly there was a segment of the capitalist class that believed this was the kind of activity which should be expanded. It seems evident, however, that there were other interests in this class who proposed alternate forms of development for the new nation. This group was composed of those who wished to see the new nation become involved in industrial production rather than confining their activities to trade and merchandising (Ryerson, 1968: 27). What is clear is the fact that all members of the business community of the day seemed to understand that the initial task in any economic development strategy was the establishment of a formally independent nation. Thus a series of steps were undertaken that culminated in 1867 with the creation of Canada.

The first government of the new nation was a coalition headed by Sir John A. Macdonald. The expansionary thrust of the new state was evident in actions such as the 1869 acquisition of Rupert's Land by the federal government and the creation of the new provinces of Manitoba and British Columbia in 1870 and 1871. By 1872, when the first general election was held, Macdonald and the Conservative Party had worked out a sufficiently coherent development scheme to win the election. The themes of industrial development, western settlement and a transcontinental rail link were emerging as dominant, the latter having been promised to British Columbia when it joined Confederation.

Following the 1872 election the Macdonald government launched a drive to have a transcontinental railway completed. This attempt by the government to encourage the development of the railway ended in failure with the famous "Pacific Scandal," as a result of which Macdonald was defeated in the 1874 general election.

The Liberal victory in 1874 was a surprise to many, including the Liberals. The new Prime Minister, Alexander Mackenzie, seems to have had difficulty in forming a government. Mackenzie and the Liberals were also philosophically skeptical when it came to massive state intervention in the economy. As a result, the new government declined to become involved in massive economic projects and this, when combined with a worldwide depression that coincided with the Liberals' assumption of power, led to a period of slower national development. The period from 1874 to 1878 was thus one of continued economic uncertainty and hardship rather than the

5

dynamic growth that some had envisioned following Confederation. As the 1878 general election approached, Macdonald and the Conservatives saw an opportunity to present the electorate with a bold scheme and they began to formulate a set of specific plans for national development that they hoped would become the basis of a successful election campaign and a new phase of Canadian development.

The National Policy

In the 1878 election Macdonald and the Conservatives were elected on the basis of his famous National Policy. Conditions for national development seemed better as worldwide economic prosperity was returning. In the North-West the land was being prepared for development as the Liberal government had begun to remove the aboriginal peoples from the land.

The Liberal government had also attempted to renegotiate the Reciprocity Treaty with the Americans, but owing to a lack of interest in the United States and the worldwide depression, it was not successful. The situation which faced Canada in 1878 was thus grim. The country was over ten years old, but the plans for development which had been devised at Confederation had failed. The western plains remained virtually unpopulated, while to the south rapid population growth was again posing a threat to the West. In the period from 1871 to 1881 the total population increase for all of Canada was only 635,000, while the period from 1870 to 1880 saw an increase of 1,123,150 in the areas of Kansas, Nebraska, Iowa and Minnesota alone. In Canada, the increase in commercial and industrial development that the Fathers of Confederation had envisioned had not occurred and therefore a drastic initiative was in order. As a result, the National Policy was formally implemented.

The National Policy that the Conservatives implemented was a three-pronged plan involving tariffs, settlement of the West, and construction of a transcontinental railway. In 1878-79 the government aggressively began to implement policies designed to bring this plan to fruition. The government was determined to implement all measures which it reckoned were necessary to stimulate national development.

A key part of the Conservative policies was a change in the nation's tariff structure. In 1878 a new tariff schedule was brought in which was much more elaborate than the former levels. Under the new schedules there were differential rates — the rates varied from 10 percent to 30 percent, depending on the amount of processing which the goods had undergone. The highest general rates applied to cotton and textiles, and steel and iron. In addition, there was no tariff on raw materials, and lower rates were placed on industrial equipment, machinery, and parts used in fabricating and industry.

Although the tariff served to benefit both the commercial and industrial interests it is commonly known as a protective tariff. The purpose of the tariff was to give developing Canadian manufacturers protection from the well-established and more technologically advanced American and English industries. The tariff also served to promote the importation of capital into the Canadian economy, a move which would generally increase economic activity to the benefit of the commercial, merchant and financial interests.

The protective tariff in place, the next problem became the enlargement of the protected markets through the creation of a new domestic market. The western regions of Canada had been secured by the Dominion government, and the process of removing the aboriginal peoples was underway; thus the area was prepared for agricultural settlement. The government had provided the basis for western settlement as early as 1872 with the passing of the Dominion Lands Act. Under the terms of this act settlers could secure title to a quarter section of land by beginning cultivation within a specified time, with the only cash outlay for the land being a nominal registration fee (Martin, 1973). The virtually free land was designed to attract to the area settlers who would produce cash crops which the eastern commercial and processing interests would refine and export. The needs of the settlers for industrial goods would also be filled by industries and manufacturers in central Canada.

There is strong evidence that politicians and business leaders had a clear understanding of the objectives of the National Policy. Moreover, they were vocal in advocating these objectives. For example, Charles Tupper, speaking in the House of Commons, indicated the essential role of the West in the National Policy:

> No person can look abroad over the Dominion without feeling that the Great North-West Territory is the district to which we must look for our strength and development. Just as the older [sic] of the United States look to their Great North-West, with its rapidly increasing population, adding hundreds of thousands and millions to their strength, not only may we look for strength by reason of an additional Customs Revenue from the increased population of that Territory, but we must look upon that western country as a field for the manufacturing industries of the older and more settled parts of Canada. Every person acquainted with this country knows we have exhausted to some extent its bread growing power, but under the National Policy that Canada has adopted, we must look forward not only to building up thriving centers of industries and enterprise all over this portion of the country, but obtaining a market for those

7

industries after they have been established; and I say where is there a greater market than that magnificent granary of the North-West, which, filled up with a thriving and prosperous population, will make its demands upon Ontario, Quebec, Nova Scotia and New Brunswick for these manufacturing products that we, for many years, will be so well able to supply. (House of Commons, *Debates*, 15 April 1880, pp. 1424-25)

Other politicians were to repeat the theme, as the following statement by Clifford Sifton in 1904 indicates:

I have to say a word as to what we expect western Canada will do for itself. But it will not be enough that it shall do only for itself. It is a portion of Canada. Canada is a national entity. Canada is an organism, and you cannot develop a single part of an organism satisfactorily. Each and all parts must contribute to the vitality of the whole. What then will western Canada do for the Canadian organism? Sir, it will give a vast and profitable traffic to its railways and steamship lines. It will give remunerative employment to tens of thousands of men, to keep the permanent way in order, to man the trains and ships, and to engage in the multitude of occupations which gather around the great system of transportation. It will do more. It will build up our Canadian seaports. It will create a volume of ocean traffic which shall place Canada in a short time in its proper position as a maritime nation. It will furnish a steady and remunerative business to the manufacturers of eastern Canada, giving assured prosperity where uncertainty now exists. These are things which the west will do for the east. In a word I may say it will send a flood of new blood from one end of this great country to the other, through every artery of commerce... (Bliss, 1966: 202-3)

A year later Sir Wilfrid Laurier spoke to the Canadian Manufacturers Association in similar terms:

They [the settlers filling up the prairie West] will require clothes, they will require furniture, they will require implements, they will require shoes — and I hope you can furnish them to them ... they will require everything that man has to be supplied with. It is your ambition, it is my ambition also, that this scientific tariff of ours will make possible that every shoe that has to be worn in those prairies shall be a Canadian shoe; that every yard of cloth that can be marketed there shall be a yard of cloth produced in Canada; and so on and so on. It does not follow that I do not want to trade with other nations, and I still hope that our scientific tariff will not prevent the trade with other nations. I want to give a preference to Great Britain, but I do not hesitate to say that I have no hard feelings against the Americans... (MacKirdy, Moir and Zoltvany, 1971: 234-35)

The plan, then, was clearly to populate the West with a population of what we might call independent agricultural commodity producers. By 1880 all the measures had been taken, or were in the process of being taken, to bring this plan to fruition. The major problem still to be solved concerned the transportation of the settlers and their supplies west and the movement of their cash crops to ocean seaports for export to the world market. The first attempt at a rail link had ended in scandal and defeat for the government in 1873, but the link was so necessary to the overall plan that another attempt was made. As a result, the Canadian Pacific Railway Company (CPR) was formed in 1880. The formation of this company and its subsequent operation have been subject to some excellent analyses (see Chodos, 1973; Gallagher, 1983), but for our purposes here we need only note in passing some of the conditions which went into the chartering of this particular corporation. Among the most important of these conditions was the granting to the company of a twenty-year rail business monopoly in the area, plus a sizeable monetary payment and land grants totalling 25 million acres. These clauses and the seeming favourable governmental treatment of the company were to become critical factors in prairie development. The important fact to be noted here is that the completion of the trans-Canada rail link in 1885 finally gave the federal government all of the instruments it needed to proceed with its plans for the development of Canada.

Success Delayed

Despite Macdonald's National Policy, from 1885 to 1900 the development of Canada simply did not take place in the fashion which the national planners had projected. From 1880 to 1900 the American population increased by about 25 percent a decade — from 50 million in 1880 to 63 million in 1890 to 75 million in 1900; during the same period the Canadian population increased by less than half as much, averaging about 1 percent per year.

An understanding of why there was not the kind of substantial development the supporters of the National Policy had envisioned requires an analysis of capitalism as a world system. A key factor inhibiting the systematic settlement of the West was the weakness of the international cereal grain market during the last decades of the nineteenth century as a worldwide recession continued to have a negative impact on commodity prices. As well, the cost of ocean and land transportation was still high, in part because of the CPR's monopoly, and this made exploitation of the Canadian West less economically attractive than the American West, where competition among railways resulted in lower freight rates. No discussion of the difficulties of establishing and maintaining agriculture on the Prairies can overlook natural difficulties — climate, the short growing season, soil — all of which were more favourable in many parts of the United States. During the period from the end of the American Civil War to 1900, one of the few areas of sustained economic development in the world was the United States and thus the lack of development in Canada is partially understood in terms of the influx of capital and labour into the United States.

By the turn of the century several changes occurred in the world economy which had a drastic impact on Canadian development. Among the central changes was the near complete occupation of the best lands in the American West which made land in Canada more attractive for settlers. In addition, changes in the costs of moving cereal grains out of the Canadian prairie region declined as a result of the Crow's Nest Pass Agreement. Finally, the price of grain on the world market rose to the point where agriculture became a profitable prospect in the Canadian West.

It is within this framework that the following analysis of western Canadian history must be placed. The importance of the National Policy for both the commercial and merchant interests of the East must be clearly understood. The fact that the National Policy was designed to serve the interests of commercial capital as well as the needs of those desiring to establish an industrial economy provided the necessary conditions for its acceptance by both of the major parties. As the century ended a Liberal government replaced the Conservatives, but the main features of the plan remained the same (Careless, 1963: 312).

The decades between the turn of the century and the Great Depression of the 1930s finally brought about the successful "completion" of the National Policy. The transportation link had been in place since 1885, the protective tariff since 1878-79, and now the third component, western settlement occurred.

The magnitude of the process can be illustrated by considering the following information. Between 1901 and 1931 the population of what is now Saskatchewan rose from just over 91,000 to over 920,000. During the same period, the number of farms in Saskatchewan increased from 13,445 to 136,471 while the total acreage covered by these farms rose from 3,833,434 acres to 55,673,460 acres.

The data available on the expansion of agricultural enterprise in Saskatchewan after the turn of the century illustrate the extent and impact of this massive immigration. We can see that Saskatchewan and western Canada were deliberately populated by a class of agricultural producers who served a number of specific functions in the Canadian economy. They were to serve as an essential market for the industrial goods produced in central Canada, while the agrarian community in the West also provided agricultural products which were handled, processed and exported by different business interests including millers, export traders and grain merchants. The settlement of the West provided a tremendous demand for credit and financing, a demand which benefited the banking and financial sector. The role of the West in the national economy has been summarized as follows:

> The decision to settle the West was part of an overall plan to develop a national industrial economy. The National Policy treated agricultural development in the West as functional, yet subordinate to this goal. The tariff policy was designed to foster industrial growth in the East; the railway policy was designed to integrate the Atlantic with the Pacific and provide transportation of goods and services across Canada. The immigration program was designed to create new markets for Canadian products in the West and to provide a new investment frontier for the East; agriculture was developed to serve an emerging industrial complex. (McCrorie, 1964: 19)

E.A. Partridge: The Early Years

An individual who was part of the process of western settlement was E.A. Partridge. He was born on 5 November 1861 on a farm near the small village of Dalston, about nine miles north of Barrie, Ontario. Few details of his early life survive other than the fact that he was one of fourteen children. Partridge attended a rural school near Dalston prior to completing secondary school at Barrie.

After completing secondary school Partridge studied for and received a teacher's certificate. He taught school for several years in Ontario but, as we shall see, he was a man of vision, restless and content only when he was a part of the building of something. The opening of the West was beckoning individuals with this spirit, and in 1883 Partridge and his brother Harry headed west, arriving in the District of Assiniboia in December. Partridge initially homesteaded a quarter section of land located north of the present town of Sintaluta, Saskatchewan. The initial homestead was on a quarter section with the legal description of NW1/4-2-18-11 W 2nd. He later moved to the SW1/4-34-18-11 where he resided until 1927.

On arrival, neither of the brothers had sufficient money to purchase the equipment and supplies necessary to take up farming. Therefore, Partridge taught school, first near Broadview and then at the Saltoun and Maple Green rural schools. His teaching activities occupied the winter of 1885. In the spring of 1885 Partridge did something that, in the view of the social, economic and political analysis he was later to develop, would appear surprising.

As settlement began to spread west the aboriginal and Métis popula-
tions were eventually forced to physically resist the encroaching
population which threatened to overrun their land and destroy the basis
of their society. The first major western resistance occurred at the Red
River Colony in 1870. In 1885 another desperate effort at resistance occurred in Saskatchewan with the second Riel Rebellion. Apparently newly
arrived settlers were told that time served in the Queen's forces would
count as residency time on their homesteads. Partridge volunteered and
joined the Yorkton Company Active Militia of Canada. There is no information concerning his actions during his period in the militia other than
that he was a private and served from 11 April 1885 to 17 June 1885.

In the course of his travels as a teacher Partridge met a young woman
from the Balcarres area, Mary Stephens. They were married in 1886, after
which time the two devoted their lives to building their farm and family.
The Partridges constructed an impressive two-storey brick house and a
large barn on "The Bluffs," as their Sintaluta farm came to be known.

In 1889 the first of their five children was born. Charles Grover Partridge was followed by May Virginia in 1892, Harold Edward in 1899,
Edna Bernice in 1901, and Enid Mary in 1908.

Since we are primarily concerned with understanding the intersection
of the life of E.A. Partridge and the historical currents that moulded and
shaped him, it is important to stress the fact that he and Mary were a part
of a remarkable historical process that saw the creation of an entirely new
population in a region of the world that was undergoing a radical and
rapid transformation. Partridge and other farmers in the West were members of a social class which many envisioned would play a pivotal role in
Canadian economic development. This was a class that had direct relationships to industrialists, grain traders, bankers and merchants, or what
we might call the various segments of the economically dominant class. In
terms of the issues raised in the introduction concerning humans as social
agents located in social structures, we can see immediately that individuals like Partridge were destined to come into direct contact with the
commercial and business interests that supported the National Policy.

What was unusual about Partridge was the fact that he seems to have
understood more clearly than many of his contemporaries the nature of
the social system of which he was a part, and its impact on him and his
contemporaries. His recognition of the existence of class, and the corresponding structure of power and domination, was the basis of his
critique of Canadian society. Prior to examining the specifics of Partridge's critique of his society, it is necessary to examine further the
precise manner in which his life story unfolded in the context of his day.

CHAPTER 2

The Emergence of the

Western Canadian Agrarian Movement, 1900

The First Shots: The Territorial Grain Growers' Association

An important aspect of human social life and existence is the presence of what sociologists call unintended consequences. By unintended consequences we mean the unexpected, unplanned, unforeseen or unintentional outcomes of our actions, words and deeds. We may develop a plan to accomplish a particular end, lay out a strategy for accomplishing that end, and undertake a series of actions to implement the strategy, only to discover that things do not work out as we had envisioned. Words, deeds and actions can be interpreted differently than had been intended, or we may find that others, for a variety of reasons, do not share the rationale that informed our ends, plans and strategies. When this happens controversies, debates and disagreements may arise when in fact we thought that the plan made "perfect sense." Such controversies, debates and disagreements may be seen as unintended consequences of our actions.

As we have seen, Canadian commercial, industrial and political leaders developed a plan to foster economic development. Under the auspices of the National Policy it was envisioned that Canada would develop into an industrial nation. The prairie region and its agrarian population were to play a central role, producing cash crops for export and serving as a captive, tariff-protected market for manufactured goods. As the West was settled and the transportation system developed, a private commercial infrastructure to handle, purchase and transport the farmers' grain was established, along with distribution networks to facilitate the sale of manufactured goods to farmers. Grain traders and merchants working hand in hand with the CPR purchased or handled the grain which farmers produced and on which their livelihood depended. Manufacturers and industrial interests utilized the same transportation networks along with an extensive regional and local retaining sector to make their products available to the agrarian community. The policy seemed to be unfolding as it should; however the reality of the subservient position of the farmers *vis-à-vis* both commercial and industrial interests soon became apparent. What emerged was one of the most important phenomena in Canadian society, the western Canadian agrarian movement. In a real sense the agrarian protest movement that developed in the West was an unintended consequence of the National Policy.

Since E.A. Partridge was to become one of the most influential figures in this movement, it is appropriate to begin our discussion of his life on the Prairies at the point at which he and other farmers began one of the first formal agrarian-based organizations in what is now Saskatchewan. The Territorial Grain Growers' Association (TGGA) was formed as a result of the problems which farmers were having with the grain-marketing system. These problems were exacerbated in the fall of 1901 when there was a record-breaking harvest in the area that is now Saskatchewan. Neither the CPR nor the grain companies were ready for the massive amounts of grain that farmers produced, and as a result nearly one-half of the crop was lost due to spoilage (Patton, 1928: 31). In addition to the grain which spoiled before it could be shipped, the poor supply of railway cars led to "plugged" elevators and farmers were unable to turn their grain stocks into much-needed income. To add to the discontent among the cash-strapped farmers, the CPR was only allocating cars to the grain companies who owned elevators, thus many farmers were unable to ship their grain directly and they had to rely on the services of the local grain merchants and handlers.

The area east of Regina around Indian Head was particularly hard hit by the acute boxcar shortage. This area was the centre of a prosperous farming community and was, at the time, one of the central shipping points for all of the North-West Territories. There were a number of farmers in the area, including Partridge, who had been discussing the need for an organization which would speak collectively for the agrarian community on important issues such as the actions of the grain trade and the CPR and even the impact of the tariff on the costs of their inputs. In late 1901 a debate was scheduled to take place at Indian Head between the Premiers of Manitoba and the North-West Territories over the annexation by Manitoba of part of the Territories. Farmers in the area felt that this would be an opportune moment to discuss some of the problems they were having, since many would be in town to listen to the debate (Moorhouse, 1918: 50), and a meeting that was to change the history of the region was called for Indian Head. Since the grain trade and manufacturing interests had organizations to advocate their concerns, the farmers decided they needed a formal organization to act as a collective voice to speak on their behalf. The result was the formation of the TGGA.

From its conception this new farm organization was careful to avoid partisan political association. Members of the two major political parties had been instrumental in organizing the meeting, and it was hoped this fact would assure the membership that the organization had no party affiliation. Many farmers feared that partisan political affiliation would doom the organization, remembering the downfall of the Patrons of

Industry after that organization entered electoral politics and became, for some, a branch of the Liberal Party. It is important to realize, however, that the movement was nevertheless political from the very beginning, since it was concerned with the broader issues of the distribution of wealth and power in society.

The initial meeting in December 1901 was followed by a period of intense work which involved establishing local organizations throughout the region in anticipation of the first convention held in Indian Head in February 1902. This convention was a harbinger of things to come as delegates directed their attention to a wide range of issues of concern to the agrarian community, though many resolutions which were passed dealt with specific business grievances of the farmers. The railways and the elevator companies received most of the attention.

E.A. Partridge was active in the TGGA from its inception. Although he was not formally a member of the administrative structure of the organization after its founding meeting, Partridge was on the Resolutions Committee at the TGGA's second annual meeting in December 1903. At that meeting he played a leading role, calling for legal action against the CPR for its failure to abide by the provisions of the Manitoba Grain Act. In his comments to the meeting Partridge expressed his concern with the manner in which government agents were handling the matter. Partridge had been told by government officials that he had to find witnesses and present the case, tasks which he felt were the responsibility of the government. In addition, Partridge noted that the officials he dealt with were "cheeky," an unacceptable attitude toward those "men who were the Sufferers." The meeting also saw the beginning of debate on an issue which would come to play an important role in Partridge's life — farmer-owned elevators.

The meeting passed a resolution requesting amendments to the Manitoba Grain Act. The proposed amendments were designed to ensure the equitable distribution of boxcars on a "first-come, first-served" basis. The farmers wanted to establish a mechanism to provide for maintaining a list at each delivery point and for the allocation of boxcars to be on the basis of one's place on the list.

Many of the resolutions passed at subsequent conventions of the TGGA were in fact brought to the attention of Parliament. During the 1902 session there were further amendments to the Manitoba Grain Act which implemented the demands of the farmers. Under these new provisions minor alterations were made in the clauses relating to the construction of loading ramps, but the crucial changes were in the methods of boxcar allocation. Under the new clauses, boxcars were to be allocated on a "first-come, first-served" basis, as had been requested.

What seemed a victory for the farm interest group soon turned out to be yet another ineffective law which the railway company ignored and which the government seemed unprepared to enforce. In the fall of 1902 there was another record crop, and again the farmers were faced with a critical car shortage. The loading ramps were of little use to the farmers, as the elevator companies were being allocated all of the cars by the CPR. The farmers appealed to the Winnipeg district office of the CPR, and were assured that the law would be obeyed, but upon returning home they found conditions were still the same. In the face of the government's seeming reluctance to take immediate action, the TGGA launched legal action against the CPR's agent at Sintaluta. The farmers won the case, which received much local and regional attention, and despite appeals to the highest court, the victory stood. As a result of this action initiated by the famers and their organization, the CPR was forced to begin allocating cars according to the provisions of the amended Manitoba Grain Act.

The victory meant a great deal to the farmers in terms of morale and their capacity to gain support for the fledgling organization: "The relief meant much to Territorial grain growers, and the Association felt that it had won a victory for western farmers that justified its organization" (Patton, 1928: 36). Moorhouse (1918: 57) comments on the reaction following the historic court battle:

> At once the newspapers all over the country were full of it. Oracles of bar-room and barber-shop nodded their heads wisely; hadn't they said that even the CPR couldn't win against organized farmers, backed up by the law of the land? Away East the news was magnified till it became: "The farmers out West have licked the CPR in court and are threatening to tear up the tracks!"

There was a period of rapid growth for the farm organization following the victory over the CPR in the Sintaluta test case, and the achievement of amendments favourable to the agriculturalists in the Manitoba Grain Act. In early 1903 there was growing demand for a similar organization in Manitoba, and with the help of Partridge the Manitoba Grain Growers' Association (MGGA) was founded in 1903. Activists in the movement spent the remainder of that year consolidating the position of the two organizations, and attempting to initiate new locals where feasible. Although the two western grain growers' organizations had no formal links, both had similar goals — the promotion of the business interests of the farmer. Under these circumstances a degree of cooperation was natural. The organizations made further representation to the federal government which resulted in additional modifications to the Manitoba Grain Act — refinements of the hastily drafted 1902 amendments.

Expanding Horizons: The Grain Growers' Grain Company

The early record of the TGGA is impressive in terms of its success in influencing the policies of the federal government in the area of grain marketing and handling. These successes soon led the farmers to broaden the range of their concerns, and as a result the basis of a much more significant social movement began to develop. As would often be the case in the subsequent years, it was E.A. Partridge who played a visionary role, raising new issues, suggesting innovative solutions, and always demanding consideration of prospects and possibilities beyond what was present at any given time.

At the TGGA's fourth annual general meeting Partridge delivered a paper entitled, "How May the Grain Growers' Association be Made More Useful and Permanent." It started by noting that the TGGA's purpose, as expressed in the constitution, was "to forward the interests of the grain growers in every honourable and legitimate way." Interests, Partridge noted, involve financial concerns, that is, profits of the members. One way the profits of the members could be enhanced was through cooperative selling. Referring to a cooperative selling venture in place in Minnesota, Partridge argued in favour of a cooperative trading association on the Prairies.

Such a bold plan of action, Partridge stated, would not only be important in addressing the grievances of the present membership, it would attract new adherents. The task of increasing membership was only one of a number of challenges which Partridge envisioned for the TGGA. Key among his other suggestions was a call for a "newspaper organ to keep our sub-associations in touch with one another and with the executive to discuss new projects, to expose abuses, to mark increases in membership and to advertise the details of the proposed Co-operative Exchange and facilitate the launching of the same." The dissemination of technical information respecting the operation of the Grain Inspection Act, grading practices, pricing, and related matters were all to be carried out by the proposed newspaper. It was to be several years before this idea bore fruit.

In his speech Partridge also began to make explicit calls for more direct political action on behalf of farmers. His first statements in this regard called on the farmers to inform the various governments about their legislative needs. In addition, Partridge called for action by farmers to inform the various government departments about their needs and concerns. In a final comment that was to prove prophetic, Partridge called for more direct political organization among the farmers:

> The members of our Association should actively participate in the selection of candidates and the formulation of the policies of their respective parties, that the agricultural class should be duly

17

represented in Parliament no matter which party reigned at the capital.

It is important to note that at this time all of Partridge's ideas and suggestions were predicated on acceptance of the basic parameters and logic of the existing parliamentary system. He was simply encouraging farmers to become more politically active and to use the means at their disposal within the existing system.

Despite numerous early legislative gains in the form of more careful government regulation and supervision of the practices of the private grain trade, farmers still had a number of concerns regarding the conduct of the grain business. Complaints about grading, weights, dockage and price fixing were still common. A particular concern which emerged was the nature of the operations of the Winnipeg Grain Exchange. In 1904 the Sintaluta TGGA local was successful in demanding that the federal government appoint a "watchdog" to observe the operation of the Grain Exchange on behalf of grain growers. The Sintaluta group further decided that more first-hand knowledge was required and Partridge was sent to Winnipeg to investigate.

Partridge arrived in Winnipeg on 7 January 1905 and stayed until 7 February. No personal accounts by Partridge himself remain to document his experiences during the month; however if Moorhouse's account is accurate it must have been a devastating experience. Partridge was treated with scorn and hostility, "made to feel like a spy in the camp of an enemy" (Moorhouse, 1918: 71), and "looked upon as a joke." Moorhouse (1918: 72) summarized his discussion of the treatment accorded Partridge:

> "Who is that fellow, anyway?" asked a grain man who had just got back to the city. He jerked his thumb over his shoulder.
>
> "Oh, *him*!" laughed his partner as he saw who was indicated. "Only that gazabo from Sintaluta who's been nosing around lately. Some hayseeds out the line sent him down here to learn the grain business. They believe that all wheat's No. 1 Hard, all grain buyers are thieves, and that hell's to be divided equally between the railways and the milling companies!"
>
> "So that's the guy — eh? — that's that man Partridge!"

Whatever the impact of the alleged treatment on Partridge, one thing is certain — he left Winnipeg convinced that the Winnipeg Grain Exchange did not operate in the interests of the real producers of wealth — the farmers — and therefore the western grain growers needed their own grain company. Partridge stopped at Brandon on the way home to address the annual meeting of the MGGA. There he spoke about the difficulties he had encountered in Winnipeg, but what was particularly important about his speech was his call for a farmer-owned, cooperative grain-handling company. Partridge noted that such an operation might eventually acquire its own elevators and even a flour mill. What was important, he stressed, was the fact that such a company would operate so as to save the producers money, and in the event that it turned a profit, that profit could be redistributed back to the membership in the form of some sort of patronage dividend (Woods, 1975: 184). The MGGA appointed a committee to study the issue with instructions to the committee to report to the next general meeting. Partridge was named chairman of the committee.

Upon his arrival back in Sintaluta Partridge drafted a letter entitled, "Shall We Co-operate to Secure Legitimate Values for Our Wheat," which he requested be read at special meetings of the MGGA and TGGA. This open letter is important because it spelled out Partridge's position in 1905 on a number of key issues, and it contains his first systematic exposition of his proposed farmers' cooperative grain company.

Partridge began by discussing the "conditions existing in the industrial, commercial and financial world today." Any student of these conditions must be impressed, Partridge argued, with the extent to which competition had been eliminated and replaced by cooperation. It is important to note that at this point Partridge equated cooperation with efforts by various classes and groups to promote their own self-interest through organization. He wrote:

> Pools, mergers, combines, trusts and monopolies are various forms
> of the co-operative principle acting with narrow limits to the benefit
> of the co-operatives and the prejudices of the outside world.

He went on to note that these cooperative efforts had been so successful that

> unless the present opportunities of those who are already wealthy be
> in some way restricted, a quarter of a century will see ninety-nine
> per cent of the wealth of North America the private property of one
> per cent of its population.

Partridge addressed what he meant by possible restrictions to the process: "Shall we look for a remedy in legislative penalties against Co-operation which makes the trusts and combines so effective for the accumulation of wealth? By no means." Rather, cooperation amongst and within the commercial, industrial and financial interests must be countered by cooperation within and among other sectors of society. Cooperation could be used as a weapon against "the financial buccaneers who employ it within narrow limits for their own enrichment." Indeed, cooperation "needs only to be universally employed to bring about an industrial millennium." In further developing the theme of the necessity to counter the growing power of large corporate cooperation, Partridge used an analogy from *Gulliver's Travels* to draw attention to the difficulties of pygmies confronting giants. The ill effect of the existing structures surely made the necessity of countering the existing power structures obvious. In his words:

> "The Beef Trust," "Standard Oil," "American Steel," "Amalgamated Coppers," "The Sugar Trust," "The International Harvest Co.," Traffic and Freight Associations, Bankers' Associations, even Traders' Unions are some of the well known giants. Already the shadow of the coming "Bread Trust" darkens the land.

> Will an Armour or a Rockefeller organize it to extort fresh billions from producers of wheat and consumers of bread alike or will the great plain people, learning wisdom from those who spoil them, organize themselves into an association that will become the sturdiest giant in the group and so restore the balance of power?

> Thus, and thus alone can the intolerable situation be done away with wherein each mighty trust, "Doth bestride the narrow world Like a huge Colossus and we petty men Walk under his huge legs and peep about to find ourselves dishonorable graves."

> The old economic conditions have passed away never to return. We must move on with the procession or be trampled underfoot.

It is important to note that at this point Partridge was in fact advocating cooperation among farmers as a means of balancing the power of business interests. He would subsequently come to the conclusion that such cooperation was in fact not appropriate because it failed to question the basic assumptions of a system based on competition and the private accumulation of wealth.

The objectives of Partridge's letter were twofold: to educate the population about the condition of society and to suggest a practical solution. The first objective should be apparent from the preceding comments. As for the second, Partridge began with a simple declaration: "there is reason to believe that the time is ripe for inaugurating the co-operative movement to the extent of forming a company of farmers to undertake the marketing of their wheat." The primary reason for this action was explicitly stated in economic terms:

> It is a well known fact that the owner of ten thousand bushels can make a much better bargain for his wheat than the owner of one thousand bushels. How much would this power be augmented in the owner of ten million bushels?

Partridge went on to lay out a direct and simple proposition:

> It is proposed to initiate the co-operative movement by organizing a

joint stock company of one thousand farmers with a capital of one quarter of a million dollars divided into one thousand shares of two hundred and fifty dollars each for the purpose of selling their principal produce — wheat — in the most economical manner and at the highest legitimate price to be obtained in the world's markets.

Safeguards would be used to prevent the company from becoming what Partridge called "the prey of capitalists." These safeguards included specification that only owners and operators of farms could hold shares, no person could hold more than four shares, one share would have one vote, and there would be limits on proxy voting.

The original proposition specified that shares would cost $250 — a considerable sum in 1906. Partridge defended this position:

The amount of a share is purposely large in order that the shareholders may represent the more successful element of the farming class. Those who have applied business principles to their private undertakings will employ them in the affairs of the corporation.

The man who is too weak financially or too lacking in moral courage to risk two hundred and fifty dollars (the price of a horse) in the endeavor to gain the knowledge and power necessary to enable him to exchange the products of his farm for the products of the forest, the factory and the mine on equitable terms is not wanted in this initial movement.

Perhaps as a result of the response he received in Brandon and the result he anticipated among members of the TGGA, Partridge recognized the innovative nature of his argument and he sought to confront the claims that he was a dreamer before they were made. He declared:

The advance guard must be brave. Our forefathers shouldered their guns and risked their lives for freedom. We their sons will scarcely refuse to shoulder a little responsibility and risk a few dollars to perpetuate that blessing.

Partridge continued to work for the establishment of a grain growers' cooperative throughout the summer of 1905. In October he and several other farmers from the Sintaluta area took the first direct steps toward the formation of the proposed cooperative when they convened a meeting to discuss the proposition. Only five farmers were present, however, they agreed to form a new company through the sale of shares valued at $250. The October meeting was followed by a much larger meeting on 27 January 1906 (Hedlin, 1960: 61).

The January meeting passed important resolutions which contain much information on the direction in which the farmers were embarking. The resolutions, which unmistakably bear the flavour of Partridge's more and more radical analysis of his society, speak of the need to counter the organized grain buyers with a farmers' cooperative. The preamble makes it clear that farmers should not seek to raise the price of bread for other "toilers" but rather work for equity and justice.

The conclusions that Partridge drew followed logically from his evaluation of the political and social dimensions of how the grain trade was organized. The fact that Partridge drew attention to the social and political side of what appeared to be a purely economic question indicates that he was thinking more and more in terms of the larger picture. Partridge assured the meeting that it was important to understand what was really happening inside the Winnipeg Grain Exchange. According to Partridge:

> The Winnipeg Grain Exchange is an institution ostensibly created to regulate and systematically prevent litigation, but is used to check, and as far as may be, extinguish, competition among its members, and conserve all the wheat business for themselves — in short it is a combine.

It was clear to Partridge that a number of nonproducer interests such as millers, shippers, elevator companies, exporters and grain merchants cooperated through the Exchange to enhance their interests.

Partridge was subsequently given an hour to speak on the issue of cooperation at the 1906 meeting in Moose Jaw. During this speech he read the long resolution which was passed at the earlier Sintaluta meeting. Partridge referred to the Minnesota Farmers' Exchange as the model for the type of company he was attempting to build, noting that the Minnesota company was involved in "the building of elevators, mills, etc. and the handling of coal, lumber and other commodities by the company." In his concluding remarks he called on the farmers to undertake decisive action:

> Farmers' Institutes, Agricultural Societies, and Grain Growers' Associations everywhere throughout Saskatchewan, Alberta and Manitoba will be *media* for advocating this movement. If you are interested, don't wait for their action. Consider yourself a committee of one to forward the movement. Send in your subscription to the Treasurer of the Committee at Sintaluta, Sask., and induce your neighbor to do likewise; and spur up the officers of any farmers' organization in your vicinity to take swift action in calling their members together discussing the project and inciting the less progressive to join this movement. If you have not a farmers' organization near you, start one.

> This is the great project. Like all great projects and all great inventions, it is simple.

> Ten thousand farmers in a company, each farmer on an average producing five thousand bushels of wheat, puts the company in

22

control of the sale of fifty millions of bushels. So simple! Why didn't somebody think of it before?

The farmers of Sintaluta have subscribed to the scheme to a man. Two hundred shares at but *one* of *hundreds* of similar points throughout the Province augurs well for the successful launching of the company. (TGGA, Annual General Meeting, 1906)

The primary objective of Partridge's work at the 1906 meeting was to develop support for the new Grain Growers' Grain Company (GGGC). Partridge was clear in his statements at the meeting that he did not want the TGGA to "father his company." Patton (1928: 47) reports that Partridge made this point even clearer in comments in the *Manitoba Free Press* in January 1907.

The spring and summer of 1906 were periods of rapid development in the life of the new company. A meeting was held in Winnipeg in April at which representatives from Manitoba and the new province of Saskatchewan met to organize a campaign to sell shares in the GGGC. The initial results of the efforts of Partridge and his colleagues were not encouraging, and less-determined individuals might not have persevered:

The voluntary canvass of the Grain Growers' Grain Company organizers in eastern Saskatchewan and western Manitoba was carried on through the spring and early summer months of 1906, with results that were the reverse of spectacular. By midsummer less than a thousand shares had been sold. In June an unexpected and disconcerting difficulty developed in the refusal of the department of the Secretary of State at Ottawa to grant the application of the farmers' company for a federal charter, on the technical grounds that the shares of a company with an authorized capital of $250,000 could not be issued at less than $100 per share par value. When the urgent representations of the organization committee's solicitor failed to obtain a reversal of the departmental ruling, the promoters suspected that secret obstructive influences were at work. In this dilemma it was decided, on Kennedy's [one of the provisional officers of the new company] suggestion, to apply to the Manitoba authorities for incorporation, although the powers of the company, contemplating, as it had, interprovincial operation, would be necessarily more restricted under a provincial charter. (Patton, 1928: 47-48)

The company was successful in its application for a provincial charter in Manitoba, no doubt in part due to the desire of the Manitoba government to maintain the support of the predominantly agrarian electorate. In the summer of 1906 the new organization set up a tent at the Winnipeg Fair, and through the publicity generated was able to secure enough support to justify the acquisition of a seat on the Winnipeg Grain Exchange. The company was still $1,500 short of the necessary $2,500 needed to secure a seat, but the matter was resolved when five of the original Sintaluta shareholders signed personal notes for the remaining funds. The company was officially inaugurated on 5 September 1906.

Although business started off rather slowly, the new company was doing well by 1 October. Moorhouse (1918: 99) states:

> Then came the bill of lading for the first carload of grain consigned to the new company, followed quickly by the second, the third, fourth, fifth, sixth — two at a time, three, ten, fifteen per day! Every foot of space in the little office was a busy spot and the lone typewriter clickety-clacked on the second-hand table with cheerful disregard of lunch hours. By the end of the month the weekly receipts had risen to one hundred cars of grain.

The success of the new company was welcome news for the agriculturalists, but not so for the grain companies operating on the Grain Exchange. The situation on the Exchange was explained by a publication of one of the farmers' companies:

> The Grain Exchange at that time was dominated largely by the big elevator companies, most of which were owned and controlled by American grain interests. These companies had been severely criticized by the farmers during the period of organization and they immediately declared war on the new farmers' company. (*Grain Growers' Record*, 1944: 7)

An attack by the established traders on the Exchange came in early October when they sent a letter to the new company summoning its representative to appear before the council to answer charges of offending the honour and dignity of the Exchange. The charges were based on a clause in the Exchange's bylaws which prohibited any member of the Exchange from rebating any portion of the commission charged back to the supplier. The GGGC was a farmer-owned joint stock company and was using the commission charges to pay a dividend to the shareholders, but it was also using some of this money as a patronage dividend. Under this technicality, the other members of the Exchange thought they could rid themselves of this new competition. Despite pleas and arguments from members of the farmers' company, including Partridge, on 8 November 1906, the GGGC was unseated from the Exchange, and an order was issued to all Exchange members stating that dealing with the GGGC would result in penalties being assessed.

In their attempts to crush the new organization by suspending its right to trade, the established corporations were nearly successful. The GGGC was faced with a situation in which it was receiving grain for which it had to pay the farmers, but which it could not sell. In a short time a large overdraft was built up at the bank and soon the bank was demanding payment. Through frantic attempts by members of the GGGC and a purchase agreement by a Scottish cooperative wholesale society, some of the grain was disposed of and the company stayed alive a bit longer.

In the meantime the MGGA intervened on behalf of the GGGC and pressured the Manitoba Premier to call a conference of all interested parties to discuss the matter. The action of the government, and concessions by the GGGC which involved termination of the patronage dividend, resulted in the reinstatement of the company's trading privileges. The pressure brought on the Exchange by the government was considerable, and included a threat to cancel the Exchange's charter if its members did not consent to allow the farmers to have their seat back.

In the period following the compromise victory of the farmers the GGGC had considerable success. In 1907 the farmers moved in another area, launching court action against the North-West Grain Dealers' Association, but the court ruled that the grain dealers were not unreasonably hindering trade, and the case was lost. In 1907-08 the volume of grain handled by the farmers' company doubled over the previous year. The Manitoba provincial government, eager to please the ever-growing farm population, passed more legislation intended to further curb the powers of the Exchange.

If we track Partridge's thinking during these struggles we begin to see the emergence of a more radical mode of social analysis than that which was typical of many members of his class. Some indication of the nature of Partridge's thought was apparent in his arguments, alluded to earlier, in favour of a farmers' grain cooperative. He elaborated his views during a speech at the 1907 annual meeting of the GGGC, subsequently published by the GGGC as a pamphlet entitled, "The Grain Growers' Grain Company Ltd. — A Farmers' Trade Union."

The speech began with an opening call to the 8,000 farmers residing between the Great Lakes and the Rocky Mountains. They were told that it was their personal responsibility to do something about "the unsatisfactory conditions which surround you, your loved ones and your fellows of the field." There were, Partridge declared, three forms of life and three related duties — community, class, and individual life duties. Participation in school meetings, mass meetings, and political meetings exemplified community duties, while taking part in the workings of agricultural societies, farmers' institutes and grain growers' associations represented class life and duties. Individual life and duties were not expounded upon as Partridge emphasized the absolute necessity of every human being to participate in community and class life. Those who failed to contribute to community and class yet who received benefits by virtue of the efforts of others were getting something but giving nothing in return, "the crime of the grafter." Still worse, such people were "setting an example of apathy, indifference and selfishness, the evil effects of which can scarcely be overestimated, since these three things are the greatest barriers to the human progress to be found in the world today."

It is in the service of community and class that human beings develop their humanity, and Partridge used a porcine analogy to illustrate his point: "A man is capable of communistic effort and self-sacrifice; a hog is a rank individualist and utterly selfish." Hogs come in a variety of kinds including the self-sufficient hog who needs no help himself and is unwilling to help others; the cautious hog is unwilling to take any risks, waiting for others to assure benefits before coming into a situation; the suspicious hog fears that those active in attempting to improve things are doing so only for their self-benefit; the apathetic hog simply wants not to be disturbed; and the meanest animal of all is the sly hog. This creature Partridge described as wholly concerned for "number one." Further, "as an office holder he is a grafter, as a voter he accepts a bribe. When the crisis is on in a class movement and loyalty is at a premium, he turns traitor... He is a strike-breaker — A SCAB."

The depths of Partridge's radical analysis and his growing commitment to the perfection of humanity were illustrated by his subsequent suggestions concerning how these "animals" should be handled: "Shall we scorn them?" he asked rhetorically. The immediate response was: "By no means." The documents which follow bring Partridge's spirituality into the analysis:

> They are our brothers — children of the same Infinite Father, but with their spiritual consciousness not yet sufficiently developed to recognize their relationship either to Him or to their fellow men.

These "animals" had the potential to develop what Partridge was to call race consciousness. By educating them, by illustrating to them the benefits of unity, of humans working together, they would come to develop their full potential.

The potential of humans to develop race consciousness was central to Partridge's lifelong political work. In this early address he defined race consciousness:

> the consciousness of absolute solidarity and complete community of interest of the human race, is a higher conception than class consciousness or a realization of the complete community interest of a class.

Class and even national consciousness are roads on the way to understanding that we are all members of the same human "race."

Turning his attention to the more immediate concerns of the membership of the GGGC, Partridge noted that the capitalist classes had long recognized the value of cooperation. Bankers, commercial interests and manufacturers had cooperated among themselves to greatly enhance their power. Indeed, these classes had been so successful that they had been able to extend their influence beyond mere economic power:

> The whole group of capitalistic classes moreover unite to control the educational system, the press and the legislative machinery to their mutual advantage. False notions of political economy are taught in the schools. Public opinion is deliberately and systematically confused and misled by a subsidized press, and legislation favorable to the "classes" and bearing heavily on the "masses," is passed by hireling legislatures.

The producing classes, Partridge argued, were learning from this example and they too were undertaking "the principle of community effort for their mutual protection and advancement." Trade unions were the result of this realization among workers, while among the farmers the lesson was manifest in the formation of a farmers' trade union — the GGGC. After discussing the merits and immediate commercial goals of the GGGC, Partridge once more illustrated the extent to which his thought went beyond the immediate. Most members of the GGGC were concerned with the more mundane issues of grain marketing, but Partridge was determined to use the issues at hand to push his colleagues into considering the broader political lessons to be gleaned from the operations of the grain market and the grain company.

Partridge insisted that any group — including farmers — had the right to resist unfair treatment:

> It is the right and duty of the farmer to refuse to sell his products for a less price than will give to him and to his family a comfortable and tasteful living, suitable clothing, healthful foods, educational opportunities ... and sufficient leisure for self culture, recreation and the performance of social duties.

By invoking this notion, Partridge opened a line of reasoning that concluded with a denunciation of the "wastes of competition and the profits of those who speculate in the necessities of life." The farmer's duties extend beyond this:

> He must, moreover, help to free industry from the exertions of those who have become possessed of the means of transportation and production. Private ownership of railways, storage facilities and natural resources must be done away with before he can enjoy even to a moderate extent the fruit of his labour.

The tasks and struggles faced by the farmers as they attempted to change the system, making it more equitable, would be difficult. External foes and apathy within the ranks of the farmers would have to be faced, but others had faced equally difficult circumstances and won, a point Partridge made with reference to labour history:

> That we have been able to maintain ourselves and grow in the face of the opposition of the monied interests on the one hand, and the apathy of the main body of the farmers on the other, is in itself no mean triumph. Look at the hardships of the engineers, miners and other classes of workers endured while their unions were in their infancy. The union men were boycotted, black-listed and starved into submission many and many a time before they became numerically strong enough to strike successfully for their rights. Gaunt men walked the streets for weeks, the mortgages on their little homes foreclosed, their wives and children destitute, but bearing it all patiently that the rights for which their husbands and fathers were struggling might be won, while capital calmly waited for hunger and want to do their work and drive the men with broken spirit back to their unremunerative toil. Such sacrifices as these are not demanded of the farmer to win *his* battle.

In his closing remarks Partridge offered more direct advice concerning specific measures that the farmers should push for, including government elevators at the local and terminal level, revisions of the practices involved in grain sampling, and the payment of advances. Partridge also noted, in an aside, that he did not believe in party government. His final remarks restated his familiar arguments in favour of continued and expanded support of and participation in the new company.

Spreading the Word: A Farmers' Press

A persistent concern of the organized farmers was the treatment they and their grievances received at the hands of the press. Partridge argued for what he called an official organ at the 1904 annual meeting of the TGGA. At that time a special committee was established to investigate the possibility of establishing a publication to represent the TGGA's views and interests. The GGGC had issued a number of pamphlets and other educational materials since its inception, and among its members there was an interest in some more formal organ. Partridge, always keenly interested in the process of education and the dissemination of information, continued to push for a publication.

An arrangement was eventually worked out between the GGGC and the MGGA to produce a monthly journal which was to be called the *Grain Growers' Guide*. Partridge was appointed the first editor, but conflict seems to have emerged over his desire to have the new journal serve both the farmers and the organized working class. Patton (1928: 71) notes

28

that Partridge wanted "to amalgamate the *Guide* with the *Voice*, the official organ of the Western trade unions." In the first issue of the *Guide*, published in June 1908, Partridge set forth the journal's purpose:

> The purpose of the *Guide's* publication is to aid in the discussion of the economic and social problems which confront us, to assist in unifying opinion among our farmers and other workers as to what it is necessary to do in order that they and we may come to enjoy to the full the fruits of our labours, and having thus unified us in opinion, to serve as a trumpet in marshalling our forces for the accomplishing of whatever has been decided is best to be done.

Patton further describes the subsequent developments in the early life of the *Guide*, noting that Partridge's view of the *Guide* met with opposition:

> This ... concept of the *Guide's* function was not shared, however, by the majority of his associates, and Partridge, burdened with other duties in the Grain Growers' movement, and ever resentful of non-concurrence with his views, resigned after the first issue. The July number never appeared. A temporary editorial successor was found, however, in Roderick McKenzie, who had been secretary of the Manitoba Grain Growers' Association since its inauguration in 1903. In the second year, it was decided to issue the *Guide* as a weekly, and an associate editor was appointed in the person of George F. Chipman, a journalist of Nova Scotia farm origin, who as legislative reporter of the *Manitoba Free Press* had shown an intelligent sympathy with the Grain Growers' movement. (Patton, 1928: 71)

Partridge's withdrawal as editor of the fledgling *Guide* followed his earlier departure as the president of the GGGC; he had stepped down at the 1907 convention and was replaced by T.A. Crerar. Apparently Partridge had been contemplating the action for some time but had been urged to retain the position until the convention. Partridge's presence as president was deemed by some to be partly to blame for the continued antagonism of the Grain Exchange toward the new company. As well, Partridge was not particularly interested in the actual commercial activities of the company, more so since its cooperative basis had been somewhat watered down in order to conform to the rules of operation of the Grain Exchange. Concern had also been expressed by some farmers who did not share his developing vision for the future of western Canada. Patton (1928: 64) summarizes the reasons for his departure:

> His motives had been so frequently questioned by Grain Growers' officers, as well as by suspicious farmers, and he had so antagonized the council of the Grain Exchange, that he felt it would be better for the company if he occupied a less conspicuous position in its direction.

The fall of 1907 brought what was to be the first of many tragedies to the Partridges. While harvesting the crop Partridge was attempting to remove tangled grain from the knife and table of his grain binder. For reasons unknown the horses bolted and his leg was nearly completely severed. He managed to crawl onto the implement and drive to the farmyard. Mary was pregnant and it seems as if Partridge's first thought was of her as he feared that she might go into shock at the sight of his injury. Their daughter reports that he shouted: "Don't panic Mary, I'm hurt but there's nothing too serious here, just a leg hanging a bit."

The leg injury proved to be very difficult in the future, and three successive amputation operations were necessary. In 1911 Partridge had to travel to Minnesota for medical attention (apparently surgery), this just a year after having visited San Antonio, Texas, for a similar reason. The expense of these treatments and the travel involved were a burden on the entire family.

New Issues: Terminal Elevators and the Partridge Plan

The departure of Partridge as president of the GGGC was not sufficient cause for the private grain trade to accept the company and the GGGC was again attacked by the Winnipeg Grain Exchange. This time the attack took the form of a cancellation of the commission policy of the Grain Exchange. Under this policy the members of the Exchange charged a fee of one cent per bushel for grain sold by them. For the grain companies which operated on the Exchange this change was possible because most had connections with local elevators and could transfer costs and profits, thereby still being able to operate on the Exchange. The move was clearly designed to attack the new farmers' company whose only source of revenue was the commission. Faced with yet another crisis the GGGC held a referendum in which 98 percent of the voters cast ballots in favour of maintaining the commission on wheat, with slightly lower rates for oats and barley. In this test of the farmers' confidence and loyalty for their company there was little doubt of the results. Patton (1928: 75) explains:

> The result of the year's trading during the suspension of the commission rule fully justified the directors' confidence in the loyalty of their shareholders. Whereas in 1908-09 the company had handled 7,643,146 bushels, its turnover in this year of "free for all" trading amounted to 16,332,645 bushels, approximately 15 per cent of the total number of cars inspected in Western Canada during the crop year 1909-10. The profits for the year exceeded $95,000.

By the end of 1909 it appeared that the farmers had won the right to market their own grain on the Winnipeg Grain Exchange through a farmer-owned joint stock company. However, this service was still available only to those who were able to sell their grain by the carload and ship it without having to deal with the local elevator. The number of farmers able to do this was limited, as many did not have a sufficient volume of grain and thus were still forced to sell to the local elevator. For these farmers the situation remained much the same as before, for they were still at the mercy of the agent in terms of grade, weight, dockage and even price since the court had ruled in favour of the Grain Dealers' Association. As Boyd (1938: 57) has noted, "notwithstanding these successes, the organized farmers had accomplished little in the way of breaking down what was generally regarded as a monopoly of elevator interests." It was against the country elevators that the next farmers' offensive was launched.

The question of government ownership of the elevator system had been a matter of debate for some years prior to its emergence as a major issue in 1909-10. At its annual meeting in 1907, the Saskatchewan Grain Growers' Association (SGGA) debated a resolution on the matter which read:

> Resolved that in the opinion of this Convention of the Grain Growers of Saskatchewan the problem of marketing the wheat crop of Western Canada can best be solved by Government control of all terminal elevators, the whole to be operated by a commission appointed by the Government, the Railway Commission and the Grain Growers of the Province, the whole cost to be borne by the grain trade.

In speaking to the resolution Partridge again eloquently laid out a series of propositions that shifted the focus of the discussion beyond the immediate issue of terminal elevators. He started by noting that his recent experiences have provided him with an opportunity to assess the shortcomings of the present system of grain marketing. A central problem with the system, he maintained, was to be found in the manner by which farmers were forced to sell their grain as soon as possible, thereby flooding the market and driving prices down. If farmers were given an opportunity to store their grain, and by using that stored grain as security to receive some income, they would be in a better position to market the grain at more opportune times throughout the year. Since this was mainly a provincial matter, Partridge stated that the logical solution would be a system of elevators at local delivery points owned and operated by the provincial government as a public service, presumably at cost. The private ownership of the terminal elevators was, Partridge suggested, a "sinister thing." The issue of private ownership of the food-processing facilities, and thus the generation of private profits based on the provision of the necessities of life, was always a concern for him.

The system which Partridge was advocating in 1907 still involved a

31

mix of government ownership and private enterprise. No mention was made of the railways other than the fact that they would benefit by a system which would spread the transportation of grain throughout the year in a more uniform manner. The government would not be involved in providing a cash advance to the farmer for stored grain; rather, the government elevator agent would merely provide a certificate to the farmer indicating the amount of grain and the grade. The farmer would then use that certificate as collateral security for loans which might be required prior to the actual sale of the grain.

As Partridge continued to develop his argument he again raised the problem caused by all farmers selling their grain within a short period of time each fall: "Would your coal merchant be accused of speculating because he put in a stoke of coal during the summer? No, but he would be a fool if he tried to sell all his coal in one month." Partridge felt that farmers needed to learn from others and spread the sale of their product out over the entire year. Further, he believed that the entire crop ought not only to be handled by government elevators but by one agency. In making this statement in 1907 Partridge previewed debates that were to take place more than fifteen years later. The convention passed the resolution.

The issue was again discussed at the 1908 convention of the SGGA. In 1908 the MGGA passed a scheme for government elevators based on Partridge's ideas. Indeed, the proposal for government elevators became known as the "Partridge Plan." The major problem addressed in the first issue of the *Guide* was this plan. The 1908 resolution passed, as did a similar motion debated at the SGGA convention in 1909. In each case Partridge played an active role, participating in the debate and extending the boundaries of the discussion to include the overall operation of the grain-handling system, as well as the entire socioeconomic system. In his closing remarks at the 1909 convention Partridge was at his best:

> This is no sordid scheme for the levying of a tribute upon the labour of others. It is part of the great struggle which the world's workers are waging against those who spoil them — a part of the world-wide protest against the vicious commercialism and industrialism based on privilege which is robbing the lives of countless millions of the share of comfort, leisure and culture which their labour has justly entitled them to. We are striving for a wider diffusion of the blessings of civilization. We want our boys to go to college, our girls to acquire those accomplishments and graces which make social contact pleasing; rest and recreation for the wives and mothers; and time for the study of life's problems and the discharge of community duties and the duties of citizenship for the fathers. It is part of the world's work we are doing. I think it is God's work as well.

Broadening the Base: Interprovincial Agrarian Cooperation

Following the establishment of the TGGA in 1901 as an agrarian pressure group, the main focus of the farmers' activity was centred on the marketing struggle. In 1907 the three major farm organizations moved to establish a coordinating body to assist in the achievement of their common goals. In that year the SGGA, the United Farmers of Alberta, and the MGGA formed the Interprovincial Council of Grain Growers and Farm Organizations. Initially the Council was not a major force in the agrarian movement, as its activities were confined to meetings of the executive officers of the member organizations designed to "formulate and harmonize policies." According to an account of the formation of the Council in the *Guide*, Partridge played a key role in its inception. Partridge saw an organization like the Interprovincial Council as a central need in the farm movement, for it would enhance the interprovincial education of the agrarian community.

In the first few years of its existence the Council acted as an agent of moral support and coordination for the various activities in which the grain growers' organizations were involved. An example of this role was the passing of a resolution at one meeting supporting the proposal originally made by Partridge for the establishment of a newspaper serving farmers' movement. The Council expressed its agreement and noted its pleasure that the company "was taking steps to finance a non-political paper which would deal fearlessly with the economic and social questions affecting the farmers' prosperity and well being" (Wood, 1975: 213).

The issues the organized farmers addressed were, of course, political in the broader sense of the word; however the Council was eager to avoid party affiliation. The Council took similar action in 1908 when it threw its support behind attempts to have the provincial governments implement the "Partridge Plan" for the public ownership of elevators. The Council made formal representation to the meeting of the three prairie premiers in 1909 at which the issue was discussed.

In 1909 there was another major development in the history of the agrarian movement. In that year plans were made to merge the Interprovincial Council with the Dominion Grange. The Dominion Grange at this time was the principal representative of the Ontario farmers. At the 1909 annual meeting of the Grange a small delegation of western farmers, including Partridge, was warmly received, and a tentative constitution was developed for a new organization which would include both the Grange and the former Interprovincial Council. The tentative constitution was presented to the various members of the Interprovincial Council and was ratified within a year. The new organization which was established was the Canadian Council of Agriculture (CCA). The purpose, the coordination of all agricultural organizations, remained the same, the major difference being the expanded membership.

From its conception the CCA was a more tightly knit organization than the former Interprovincial Council had been. The constitution of the CCA set forth the objectives of the new organization in concise form. The CCA sought to:

> stimulate organization among the farmers of Canada; to collect data from a variety of sources for the organized farmers' use; to facilitate their demands for legislation; to encourage their interest in political matters so that their views might be given proper representation; and to urge the advisability of co-operative methods of purchase and sale. (Boyd, 1938: 59)

In addition to spelling out the objectives of the new organization, the new constitution also stipulated what organizations were eligible for membership. Membership was open to "any association of farmers that was prepared to give effect to these objectives and that was entirely independent of government control."

Keeping Up the Pressure: Local and Terminal Elevators

The agitation from the new organization and others in favour of government intervention in the elevator business became strong enough to warrant a conference of the three prairie governments in Regina in May 1908. At this conference the prairie premiers proposed no basic changes in the grain-marketing structure. They suggested that elevators remain in private hands, but that profits should be controlled. The premiers also suggested grain-grower supervision of certain elevator operations, and the establishment of more storage and loading facilities by the CPR to assist in removing the major evils of the system. The agrarian response to the proposals was lukewarm. The retention of the elevators by the grain companies was felt to leave the problem untouched, and the government had been urging the CPR to provide better facilities for years. The *Grain Growers' Guide* summarized the farmers' response by remarking that farmers had asked for an apple and "not a turnip instead."

The farmers who were not satisfied with the first conference arranged another, which the three premiers again attended. The farmers proposed government ownership of the elevators, and the premiers, in a clever political move declared themselves in support of the idea. The political agility of the premiers was further demonstrated by the fact that they stated that although they supported the idea, they could not act, claiming that such a matter was beyond their constitutional powers and thus would require federal government action. The Interprovincial Council claimed the matter was indeed within the powers of the provincial governments, since the Council was not requesting total government takeover, but merely that the governments enter the field to provide an alternate system of conventional elevators.

In the meantime the political parties sensed a need to move on the issue. In Manitoba a by-election was held and a farmers' candidate was victorious. In that contest a major issue was government ownership of the elevators. This event, plus the continued pressure of the agrarian community in the form of petitions and delegations, led the Manitoba government to announce its plans to establish an internal line of elevators as a public utility. In the meantime, Saskatchewan established a royal commission to examine the proposals of the SGGA regarding the establishment of an alternate system of elevators.

Since the Manitoba government was the only prairie government to become involved in the government ownership of elevators, the results of that endeavour were watched very closely. In Saskatchewan, concern was raised that this sort of operation could possibly be used by "a government that wanted to discredit the whole principle of public ownership" (Wood, 1924: 213). Although it appears that there is no evidence that this was the case, events during the two-year operation of the plan cast doubts, in the minds of some farmers at least, of how sincere and committed the Manitoba government was to the scheme. The government chose the president of the MGGA to head a commission that oversaw the operations of the elevator system. Wood reports that this chairman endured the "dictation" of the government "manfully" but was eventually forced to oversee the closing down of the government elevators because they were loosing money (Wood, 1924: 220).

The Manitoba scheme seems to have been doomed to failure, for the government-operated elevators were to be used as storage and loading facilities only and, as has been noted, many farmers were forced to deal with elevators which would purchase their crops for immediate cash. Other factors, such as the purchase of elevators which had a history of poor volumes, or elevators in poor physical condition gave the government elevators a serious handicap. Farmers in Manitoba were fully cognizant of the reality of the situation as their representative on the House Agricultural Committee stated: "If you are fully determined to carry out your scheme, while we are sorry to say so, we cannot assume responsibility in connection with it, because we feel it would be a failure" (Boyd, 1938: 59).

After two unsuccessful years of operation the Manitoba plan ended in failure. The Manitoba premier declared that he had been wrong to listen to the farmers, claiming they did not want a publicly owned elevator system because the plan had failed. As a result of its failure, the government sought to turn the elevator system over to the grain growers themselves. In early 1912 negotiations were conducted which resulted in the leasing of the government elevators by the GGGC. In the first year of operation the company lost money, but after three years the margin had changed to a $161,608 profit (Patton, 1928: 97). The company's success once it was able to purchase grain is illustrated by the fact that it was able to purchase terminal elevators in 1913 at both Fort William and New Westminster.

As was noted above, Saskatchewan established a royal commission in late 1909 to study the elevator question. The commission reported its findings in 1910 and, despite substantial farm pressure to the contrary, rejected government ownership such as had been attempted in Manitoba. Instead, the commission recommended a grain growers' cooperative elevator system which would receive some initial financial assistance from the government. Legislation to set up the Saskatchewan Co-operative Elevator Company was subsequently introduced into the provincial legislature in the following session.

The provisions of the legislation which set up the new farmers' company provided for the establishment of a form of joint stock company. The shares were to be priced at $50 each, and no farmer could hold more than ten shares. The legislation stipulated that when enough shares had been sold in an area to cover the capital cost of the construction or acquisition of an elevator, such steps could be taken. There were no contracts which bound members to trade with the company, but as it was their company, the provision for payment of patronage dividends according to volume of business made it more attractive. The record of growth of the company speaks for itself:

> At the date of the second annual meeting at Regina on November 10, 1913, the number of farmer shareholders had risen from the 2,508 reported at the first general meeting in July, 1911 to 13,156, grouped in 192 locals — more than a five-fold increase. The Saskatchewan Co-operative Elevator Company had undoubtedly taken root throughout the province. (Patton, 1928: 111)

In spite of the success of the farmers' elevators at the local level the grain which the farmers shipped still had to pass through the privately controlled terminal elevators, where it was loaded for shipment to the final destination. Initially there were three terminals operating at Port Arthur. One of these was owned by the CPR, the other two by milling companies. The farmers' complaints against the terminals included the old issues of mixing of grades, incorrect weighing, and storage charges being levied for grain already shipped. In addition, there was general distrust due to the fact that the companies who owned the terminal elevators were also owners of local elevators, and this tended to strengthen their monopoly position. In their "Siege of Ottawa" in late 1910, the question of the terminal elevators was one of the issues which the farmers raised.

As the terminal elevator question was crucial to the agrarian West, and as the federal government was still attempting to facilitate settlement and stability in that area, a special Senate Committee studied the matter. As a result, a new grain bill was introduced in 1911, but the House was dissolved before the bill was passed. Following the election of the Borden Conservative government on a platform which the agrarian community viewed with hostility, the government undertook to do whatever it could do to pacify the western farmers.

As a first step in this direction the Conservative government passed the Canada Grain Act in 1912. This new bill superseded the old Manitoba Grain Act. The farmers had been advocating the establishment of a system of government-owned terminal elevators, but the government was not prepared to go that far. The new Grain Act did, however, meet some of the farmers' grievances. Among the main clauses were allowances for the creation of a Board of Grain Commissioners to supervise all aspects of the grain trade, tighter regulations regarding the mixing of grain, formal provision for government-owned terminals, and a prohibition against companies operating both country elevators and terminal elevators.

As had been the case earlier when the government refused to nationalize the local elevators, the grain growers now moved to secure for themselves the terminal facilities they needed. Negotiations were conducted between the GGGC and the CPR to lease the terminal the railway company was operating at Port Arthur. These negotiations were successful and the GGGC took over this terminal elevator in 1912. There were drawbacks to this arrangement, as the acquired elevator was only a storage and loading facility, so the company acquired another terminal elevator in 1913 which was equipped to clean and condition grain.

New Ventures: The Square Deal Grain Company and the Home Bank

In the years preceding World War I the GGGC expanded its operations considerably. In 1912 the GGGC, which initially had been refused federal incorporation, made a successful attempt to secure a federal charter. In the new charter permission was given to the company to diversify its activity into merchandising, manufacturing, and resource development in areas not directly associated with agriculture. The company was quick to act, expanding into the merchandising area in 1913 with the organization of the Co-operative Supply Department. Initially this new company began supplying farmers with commodities such as coal, flour, feed, and even apples. In 1914, the GGGC attempted to expand into the farm machinery supply business. Owing to the fact that the major machinery producers refused to supply the farmers with machinery to distribute, the GGGC found it necessary to make deals with smaller American firms. After an initial period of difficulty, the GGGC established a warehouse for better parts distribution, and was able to carry on a profitable business (Patton, 1928: 291).

By the second decade of the century, two separate farmer-owned companies involved in the grain trade were operating in Saskatchewan. The GGGC had diversified its operations to a considerable degree, while the Saskatchewan Co-operative Elevator Company had concentrated on the establishment of local elevators. There was some concern over the possibility of rivalry between these farmer-owned operations. In addressing the 1914 annual conference of the GGGC, T.A. Crerar, then president, stated:

> With the development of the Saskatchewan Co-operative Elevator Company, and now the Alberta Co-operative Elevator Company, we must not ignore the possibility of misunderstanding, jealousy, and difference of opinion arising. I say it boldly, that it is the business of the men connected more closely with the guiding of the destinies of these concerns, to build and mould them on harmonious lines. The interests of the farmers of Western Canada, individually or otherwise, are in all essentials the same. (*Grain Growers' Record*, 1944: 17)

The interest in some sort of merger among the various farm cooperative companies was stronger among those associated with the GGGC than with those of the Saskatchewan Co-operative Elevator Company. The relative position and structures of the two companies explain this fact. The GGGC, from its inception, was a joint stock company whose initial centre of activity was located in Winnipeg. The individual shareholders were thus not constituted around a local unit, as was the case with the Saskatchewan Co-operative Elevator Company. The GGGC had found that many of its shareholders were satisfied to draw their dividends without concerning themselves with the operation of the company and, in some cases, without even contributing their patronage. It was therefore hoped that the merger with the more cooperatively structured elevator company would result in the GGGC becoming more of a cooperative venture. The GGGC was also at a disadvantageous position in the competition with the other farmers' grain companies, particularly the Saskatchewan Co-operative Elevator Company. The latter company had a much larger network of local elevators, and since its second year of operation had its own seat on the Grain Exchange. The GGGC, while retaining its seat on the Exchange, did not have a complete network of local facilities.

In November 1915, at the annual meeting of the GGGC, a resolution was passed requesting the directors of the company to seek federation of the various farmers' organizations. Following this directive a meeting was held early in 1916 at which time federation of the Saskatchewan and Alberta Co-operative Elevator Companies and the GGGC was discussed. It was proposed that the GGGC be the central marketing and supply agency while the cooperative elevator companies would maintain their local elevator business. There was dissent at once from the Saskatchewan Co-operative as it did not want to give up its lucrative seat on the Winnipeg Grain Exchange. Negotiations with the Saskatchewan Co-operative continued but without success. The GGGC and the Alberta Farmers' Co-operative Elevator Company did, however, amalgamate at the end of the 1916-17 crop year. The new company, the United Grain Growers (UGG) took over the combined business of the two on 1 September 1917.

Partridge may have felt ambivalent about the commercial success of the GGGC and subsequent formation of the UGG. While he had strenuously argued for joint, cooperative commercial actions among the farmers during the period of the formation of the GGGC, the nature of his social, political and economic analysis had changed considerably by 1912. In that year he resigned from the board of directors of the GGGC because of his increasing concern with the direction the company was taking. Partridge was concerned even prior to his resignation as president in 1907 that the company not become simply another commercial operation. The continued radicalization of his thinking led to his formal resignation from the board in 1912.

Partridge not only resigned from the board of the GGGC, he also attempted to set up an alternate company which he hoped would be true to the principles of cooperative existence. Called the Square Deal Grain Company, it was registered on the Winnipeg Grain Exchange under the name of W.E. MacNaughton from 1912 to 1915; it existed as a registered company for the years 1914-15.

Partridge was a visionary thinker unwilling to accept that the situation at any given moment was all that was possible. He always had an eye on the future while criticizing the present for its failure to live up to its possibilities. Apparently, it was the failure of the GGGC to live up to the possibilities that Partridge had envisioned for it that was behind his decision to found the Square Deal Grain Company.

In a communication dated 20 September 1912, Partridge explained some of the reasons for his decision to disaffiliate himself from the GGGC and start the new company. He started by noting that: "The excuse, which the Grain Growers' Grain Company has for its existence is that it is improving conditions surrounding the marketing of the grain and providing an avenue for the sale of grain satisfactory to the farmer shipper."

Although the company had improved the situation of the farmer, Partridge went on to observe "that the major part of this work of unifying has been accomplished by myself rather than those who are in charge of the destinies of the company." His dissatisfaction with the increasingly commercial orientation of the company was apparent:

My dream, as an organizer of the Grain Growers' Grain Co. was to see the company provide an entirely dependable medium for the passage of the grain from the farmer to the hands of the ultimate user with the least circumlocution and cost. Second that the profits of the business would be divided co-operatively in order to reduce the expense to the farmer to the actual cost, after providing for his advantage in educational and other ways. I sought to make the *Grain Growers' Guide* the official organ not alone of the three provincial farmers' associations, but also of Organized Labour. I had in fact nearly completed an arrangement for the amalgamation of *The Guide* and *The Voice*, when interfered with by a narrow spirit of jealousy on the part of the farmers toward the workers in the town. I was particularly anxious that the work of the company should include the export business. Now, through the folly of the management, the credit of the company with financial institutions has been so impaired that they are not able to finance an export business. The condition of being supplied with credit this year involves, as I happen to know, an abandonment of all activity in the direction of export.

A key part of the "folly of management" referred to was, in Partridge's opinion, the manner by which the company operated on a day-to-day basis. Partridge listed a number of practices which he claimed the company had engaged in and which he felt were totally inappropriate for a farmers' cooperative. Included in the list of inappropriate actions were specific practices such as ignoring the instructions of the farmer shippers, charging 6 percent interest for loans on grain already in storage, and charging farmers for grain in storage which had already been sold. In a later communication seeking business for the new company, Partridge further explained his reasons for embarking on the new endeavour:

Feeling that the methods and management of the Grain Growers' Grain Company were no longer such as to entitle that institution to be regarded as any more interested in the well being of the farmer than any other corporation, or any more likely to improve undesirable conditions or practices in the grain trade, a number of men who had been prominent in organizing it decided to create the Square Deal Grain Company and to retain the management in the hands of those who would keep absolute faith with their patrons.

Partridge then went on to restate his earlier claims that the GGGC had "departed from the ideals of its founders, engaged in speculation, took advantage of the loyalty of the farmers to retain their support after having ceased to deserve it, and in a number of ways abide their confidence." The letter documents these charges and ends with a request for support.

Few details of the actual operation of the Square Deal Grain Company survive. It seems to have ceased operating in 1915, since a letter dated 6 August from the GGGC to Partridge refers to the winding down of the Company. By this time the rigours of attempting to operate another company as well as an apparent change of heart seem to have altered Partridge's position. The letter makes it clear that the GGGC was to assume operation of the Square Deal Grain Company, its assets and the business of its patrons. Partridge even provided a letter to the GGGC which was aimed at the Square Deal Grain Company's patrons, urging them to transfer their business to the GGGC.

There is evidence that the Square Deal Grain Company was linked to another venture instigated by Partridge, a cooperative store in Sintaluta. Again, details of the operation are not available, but there is evidence that it was to be called the Farmers' Cash Store (Saskatchewan Archives Board-Regina, Tape A-982, 983).

Partridge was involved in another unsuccessful venture in his tireless efforts to improve the lot of the western farmer. In the early years of its existence one of the difficulties faced by the GGGC was securing the support of a bank to assist in financing its operation. The company arrived at an arrangement with the Bank of British North America, but in 1907 that institution informed the GGGC that it intended to close the company's account. However, the manager of the bank's branch in Winnipeg came to the assistance of the GGGC. Patton describes the process:

> The Winnipeg manager of the Bank of British North America, Mr. W.H. Machaffie, had always been sympathetic to the Grain Growers' Company, and shortly after the receipt of the headquarters notification, he resigned from that bank to undertake the Winnipeg management of the Home Bank, an eastern institution which had evolved from a loan and savings company into a chartered bank, and was now seeking to establish itself in the expanding Western field. Machaffie at once sought the Grain Growers' account for the new bank, and the company's line of credit was assured for the new crop movement.
>
> The financial arrangements between the young bank and the young grain company were soon carried beyond the mere relations of lender and borrower. The Home Bank was anxious to increase the number of its Western shareholders. The Grain Growers' Grain Company, on the other hand, was desirous of securing some measure of control in a bank which was known to be less directly identified with the larger

capitalistic interests. It was felt that a bank in which farmers were substantial stockholders might reasonably be expected to show greater consideration to the credit requirements of both the farmers' company and individual farmers. (Patton, 1928: 65-66)

The decision by the company and many individuals including Partridge to tie up money in the Home Bank proved to be disastrous. The Home Bank itself had its head office in Toronto. It grew out of the Home Savings and Trust Company and during its twenty-year life (1903-23) had branches in most major cities and many smaller towns. Rumours of difficulties in the bank began to circulate as early as 1914 but the government was unwilling to take any action, fearing the repercussions of a bank failure or reorganization during wartime. By 1923, however, the Bank was forced to suspend operations, an outcome that was to cost Partridge and others dearly.

At one time the GGGC had 1,000 shares in the Home Bank but these had been sold prior to the failure. Partridge and others were not so fortunate and many shareholders ultimately faced double liability — not only did they lose their shares, but as shareholders they had some responsibility for the deposits of others. Partridge organized The Home Bank Shareholders Protective Association which collected a fee of $1.00 and was able to get legal advice, which apparently saved many shareholders considerable money. Partridge himself lost a considerable sum of money; indeed, his personal loss jeopardized his marginal farming operation.

Despite his frequent criticism of the company, the GGGC came to Partridge's assistance and saved his farm. The directors, in appreciation of Partridge's efforts through the years, decided to liquidate his obligations to the bank and remitted to him an amount of cash. The total allotted to the transaction was to be $5,000. Partridge's obligations to the bank were in excess of $4,200 — an enormous sum at that time. Partridge received a cheque from the GGGC for over $772. In a letter thanking the directors, Partridge acknowledged that without the assistance he would have had to sell his farm and move. He noted that the help had arrived at a moment of near despair for him. His concluding comments tell of his deep optimism: "Now I am filled with hope — itself a good mental restorer — of our being able to keep the old farm and having it keep us."

A New Marketing Crisis: Wheat Board or Wheat Pool?

Returning briefly to developments unfolding on the grain-trade front, following the establishment of the UGG, the pressures and disruptions of wartime grain marketing led to the establishment of the Board of Grain Supervisors. This body served primarily a regulatory function, coordinating the sale of the entire surplus of Canadian grain to the joint allied grain purchasing agency. For the crop years 1917-18 and 1918-19, the

42

Royal Commission on Wheat Supplies fixed the price at which the crop was to be sold. During this period the operations of the Winnipeg Grain Exchange were temporarily terminated.

Following the war many Canadian farmers opposed the reopening of the Grain Exchange for they felt that the state of instability that remained in the European market, plus the American retention of a government-controlled wheat market, would result in excessive speculation. The farmers were correct: between 22 and 28 July 1919, the price of wheat went from $2.24 to $2.45 per bushel. The federal government closed the market on 28 July 1919 and established the first Canadian Wheat Board. Its purpose was to hold the price of wheat down.

While grain marketing was under the control of the Canadian Wheat Board, the operations of the Grain Exchange at Winnipeg were again suspended. The grain handlers received grain and forwarded it to the Board's "account." The Board fixed an initial price which the producers received at the time of delivery. The producers also received a "grain ticket" or certificate registering the quantity of the delivery. After the crop year the profits made by the Board were returned to the producers on the basis of their deliveries in the form of the "final payment." Although there was some dissent when the Board was established, since its purpose had been to hold prices down, the high returns which farmers realized on the crop the Wheat Board marketed led many to demand its retention.

Opposition to the maintenance of this government price guarantee was mounting, however. Among the chief opponents were those who were prevented from realizing profits through the open-market system, the grain trade and the milling interests. Consumers in eastern Canada also opposed the Wheat Board because they felt it was responsible for the higher prices they were paying for grain products.

In July 1920 the Canadian government announced that it was not legislating the continuance of the Wheat Board and the Winnipeg Grain Exchange resumed operations on 18 August 1920. In the period following the reestablishment of the open market, the price of wheat declined drastically (see Table 1). The government had inadvertently demonstrated the value of pooling production and receipts for independent commodity producers, and the period following the decision to reestablish open marketing was one of intense agrarian demands for a return to government control in grain marketing.

The reaction of the Canadian Council of Agriculture (CCA) to the drastic drop in wheat prices was to demand the immediate reestablishment of the Wheat Board. Failing this, the CCA had other plans. The Farmers' Platform issued earlier had mentioned the possibilities of cooperative

43

Table 1	
Average Price of Saskatchewan Spring Wheat	
Year	Average Price for Year ($)
1918	1.99
1919	2.32
1920	1.55
1921	.76
1922	.85
1923	.65
Source: Saskatchewan Dept. of Agriculture Annual Reports, 1918, 1920, 1922	

marketing, and now, with the government refusal to reestablish the Wheat Board, the farmers began to take it upon themselves to organize a pool which would handle the grain in a fashion similar to the former Wheat Board. In October 1920 the CCA established a committee to study the matter. Following its report in December of that year, the Grain Marketing Committee was established.

As the farmers began to consider the idea of a producers' pool, the idea of the Wheat Board did not die. During the same time that the pool idea was gaining strength, there was still considerable support for the demands that the Wheat Board be reestablished:

> However, at a meeting of the Executive [of the SGGA] held in the month of December, 1921, it was resolved that the association's delegates to the Canadian Council of Agriculture be instructed to request the Council to use its utmost endeavour to persuade the new government to re-instate the Canada Wheat Board to handle the crop of 1922, and until such time as world conditions again would become normal. The SGGA convention of 1922 also demanded the re-instatement of the Wheat Board. (Yates, 1947: 38)

The federal government responded to these demands by declaring that it could not reinstate the Wheat Board since it no longer had the power to do so. The first Wheat Board had been established when wartime powers were still in effect. The federal government proposed that the prairie provincial governments operate a wheat board, and went so far as to pass the necessary federal legislation. The legislation required the support of two of the three provinces, but neither Alberta nor Manitoba shared the interest of Saskatchewan since their economies were not as dependent on wheat production. In 1922 Saskatchewan passed the necessary legislation, but because the plan appeared to have marginal chances of success, due to the unenthusiastic attitudes of the other provinces, the personnel needed to manage the board could not be found. Saskatchewan and Alberta were prepared to support the idea of the board, but only as a temporary measure until a voluntary pool could be established. Manitoba rejected the idea altogether.

A New Farmers' Union

The drive for the establishment of the Wheat Board, and then the wheat pools, was the last major activity in which the Canadian Council of Agriculture was involved. In 1921 the formation of the Farmers' Union of Canada, Saskatchewan Section, brought into existence another organization with similar purposes and functions. The CCA faded into the background, and in 1930 was officially disbanded. The idea survived, however, and in 1935 it was revitalized under the name of the Canadian Chamber of Agriculture, which became the Canadian Federation of Agriculture in 1940.

In 1921, the Farmers' Union of Canada, Saskatchewan Section, was organized following a difference of opinion on how best to solve marketing problems. In the opinion of the founders, the SGGA was too involved with the local Liberal party and the Saskatchewan Co-operative Elevator Company to retain a proper perspective on the marketing issue (McCrorie, 1964: 31-32). In 1926 the Farmers' Union of Canada merged with the SGGA and formed the United Farmers of Canada (UFC), Saskatchewan Section.

The enormous contribution of Partridge to the farmers' cause and farmers' movement was recognized by the UFC, Saskatchewan Section at its first annual meeting. After the election of an executive the following resolution was passed:

> Whereas Mr. E.A. Partridge during the course of a long life has unfalteringly and energetically led the forces in the field for the betterment of social relations;
>
> And whereas all through the long years of struggle his behaviour has been characterized by absolute unselfishness, in that he has never striven for personal advancement either officially or financially, thus setting a mark of high endeavour that will be an inspiration for all members of society in this and succeeding generations to emulate;
>
> And whereas we the admirers and comrades of Mr. E.A. Partridge are desirous of some tangible evidence of our love and respect being shown to him;
>
> Therefore be it resolved that this initial meeting of the U.F.C., Sask. Section, in Convention assembled, go on record as being in favour of some suitable testimonial being prepared together with any other suitable recognition as may be suggested, and the same presented to Mr. E.A. Partridge with the least possible delay.

45

Immediately following the passage of this motion the position of Honorary President was created and E.A. Partridge was elected for a period defined as "the life of the United Farmers of Canada." Despite his physical absence from the region and his failing health, Partridge sent messages to both the 1930 and 1931 annual meetings of the UFC.

The Drive for Wheat Pools

The Farmers' Union of Canada's drive for the establishment of a voluntary contract pool began at once. As the Saskatchewan supporters of the pool idea spread the word in neighbouring Alberta, the United Farmers of Alberta sought the assistance of Aaron Sapiro, an American lawyer who had worked organizing various sorts of pools in the United States. The Alberta drive culminated in the establishment of the Alberta Wheat Pool, which began operations in the fall of 1923. Efforts in Saskatchewan to establish an operating pool the same year failed when the required acreages were not signed up, but as Yates (1947: 86) notes, it was only a "temporary setback." Through a massive effort by local leaders, and a speaking tour by Sapiro, the required acreages were under contract on time for the operation of the pool in the 1924 crop year.

During the period of debate and turmoil over the pool versus board solution, the situation was further confused by the presence of two organizations both claiming to speak for farmers — the Farmers' Union of Canada and the SGGA. In the process that produced the successful formation of the first wheat pool, the two groups had worked together. In the "sign up" drive which preceded the formation of the pool the members of both organizations had cooperated to bring the campaign to a successful conclusion. There were problems, however:

> For, while the Saskatchewan Grain Growers' Association and the Farmers' Union had united their forces for the purpose of the organization of the Pool, they still maintained their separate educational organizations, with the inevitable friction and ill-feeling that competition for membership was bound to perpetuate. (Yates, 1947: 136)

The potential harm to the pooling movement was thus one of the factors that led to the merging of the two organizations.

Despite the considerable tension between the SGGA and the Farmers' Union prior to the merger, the new organization presented a solid front. Between 1927 and 1931, during the debate on the compulsory pool, the membership of the UFC presented the strongest support for the plan, eventually leading the badly split pool membership to accept the proposal. Frequently, the "brain child" of the parent organization replaces the parent, and in the case of the UFC and the Saskatchewan Wheat Pool this is what happened. The movement of the pool into the education field led to a situation in which the two organizations were attempting to accomplish the same end. The actions of the UFC as one of the founders of the CCF in the early 1930s, plus the entrance of the pool into the field of education, led to the temporary decline of the UFC. In 1948 the organization's name was changed to the Saskatchewan Farmers' Union. This organization operated in Saskatchewan until 1969 when it, along with three other provincial farm unions, merged to form the National Farmers' Union.

As noted, the demand for the establishment of some sort of producers' pool had been growing, becoming one of the central purposes for the creation of the Farmers' Union in 1921. In 1923, following the collapse of provincial attempts to establish a wheat board, the pool idea gained even more strength. In that year concerted attempts were made in Saskatchewan and Alberta to form a pool. In August, the Saskatchewan Co-operative Wheat Producers Limited was incorporated, but it was not as successful as the attempt in Alberta where, in the fall of 1923, a wheat pool began operations. In Saskatchewan the recruitment of farmers into the pool fell short of the necessary number and the plan had to be postponed for a year. In the summer of 1924 the Farmers' Union utilized the services of Aaron Sapiro to convince farmers to sign pool contracts. The second drive was a success and the pool began operations in the fall. In the same year there was a successful attempt to organize a pool in Manitoba, and the operation of wheat pools in all three prairie provinces led to the establishment of a central sales agency with federal incorporation — the Canadian Co-operative Wheat Producers Limited. The first year of operation for the new Saskatchewan pool was a success.

During the first year of operation the pool in Saskatchewan utilized the services offered by the other farmers' elevator companies for handling the pool's grain. In this situation, the pool found itself at a disadvantage since it had no representative at the key point in the chain — the producers' sales point. The contracting of agents of other organizations to handle the grain also had its drawbacks:

> However conscientiously the agents of the co-operative or other elevator companies might carry out the terms of the contract governing the handling of pool wheat, their primary responsibility was to secure grain for their own principals, and to forward it as promptly as possible to terminal position. Even if not unfriendly to the pool, they were hardly likely to be interested in promoting the smooth running and the extension of the pooling method in their locality. (Patton, 1928: 228-29)

Given these problems and limitations, the pool moved in 1925 to begin acquiring elevators. In that year Saskatchewan Pool Elevators Limited was established as a subsidiary of Saskatchewan Co-operative Wheat Producers. In acquiring elevators, the pool initially sought to purchase or build elevators at points not served by the existing farmers' companies, but this policy was soon abandoned (Patton, 1928: 233).

From the formation of the Territorial Grain Growers' Association in 1901 to the establishment of the pools in the mid-1920s, Partridge was an important player in a series of radical transformations of the Canadian grain trade. Bitter experience convinced many farmers that they could not and would not receive honest, much less equitable, treatment from some elements of the grain trade. Various federal governments sought to appease the demands of the farmers for regulation and supervision of the grain trade; however, the farmers determined that it was within their power to alter the structures of the system and they took it upon themselves to do just that. As we have seen, Partridge was a central actor in many of the cooperative ventures through which the agrarian community fundamentally altered the nature of the grain trade. As important as the grain trade was, it was not, as we shall see, by any means the only issue which Partridge and other members of the agrarian community sought to redress through collective action.

CHAPTER 3

The Second Great Issue: Farmers and the Tariff

The Debate Emerges

One of the issues that was to occupy more and more of Partridge's attention and thought was the question of the role of the state and the nature of political power in a society such as Canada. As we have seen, as Partridge attempted to change the nature of the grain trade and the grain-handling system, he became more and more interested in the issue of power and control in society. By the mid-1920s, he concluded that Canada was not really a democratic society because of the manner by which those classes with economic power were able to exercise political control. Why did he arrive at this conclusion? By attempting to understand the context of his evolving and developing political viewpoints, we are better able to understand how an individual such as E.A. Partridge moulded and was moulded by his society. We are able to glimpse the historical context in which Partridge's political views developed by examining *the* central political issue for members of his class during the first three decades of this century — the tariff debates.

The overview of the National Policy presented in Chapter 1 illustrates that prairie farmers were to play a vital role in the industrialization process in Canada by serving as an expanding tariff-protected market for Canadian industry. We know that the establishment of an agricultural frontier was an integral part of the National Policy and it was via the protective tariffs that this market was to be "protected" in the interests of Canadian industry. Though the tariff might have protected the captive western market for the benefit of those with capital invested in manufacturing plans in central Canada, for the settlers and farmers in the West, the tariff meant higher prices for the manufactured goods they required. Under such circumstances there was, not surprisingly, an abiding interest in tariff policy in the region.

Though the system of protective tariffs associated with the National Policy had been implemented by a Conservative government, after the Liberals assumed power in 1896 they adopted the tariff as their own. As early as 1899, western members were raising the issue of the tariff in the House of Commons and demanding reform, meaning tariff reductions. On 26 June 1899, the member of Parliament for West Assiniboia, Nicholas Flood Davin, demanded the removal of tariffs on farm machinery, claiming that farmers were being "bled white by the manufacturers" (House of Commons, *Debates*, 1899, p. 5869). The debate continued, as after the turn of the century the Canadian Manufacturers Association (CMA) began to pressure the government for even higher tariffs, an action that produced a negative response from farmers. The issue of tariff policy was taken up at various farm meetings and was kept alive in the pages of the *Guide*.

The Great Reciprocity Debate

The issue took on new importance in 1910 when the American government approached Ottawa with a request to enter into negotiations aimed at lowering tariffs. As this process unfolded, Prime Minister Laurier embarked on a tour of western Canada. Farmers used their organizations to articulate their demands for lower tariffs to Laurier, presenting him with numerous petitions and resolutions at virtually every stop on the Prairies.

The *Guide* was quick to respond to these tariff discussions. In its lead editorial in the 18 May issue, the *Guide* stated that it was "high time" that a Prime Minister visited the West on a formal tour. The *Guide* pointed out that Laurier was once a free trader and the tour would be an opportunity for the people of the West to express their tariff views with an eye to changing Laurier's present position. The next issue's lead editorial, "Our Great Opportunity," continued the theme, stressing the need to convince Laurier to act on a number of concerns including government ownership of elevators, the tariff, and the Hudson Bay Railway. The editorial ended by noting that "For the first time in 14 years the Premier of Canada is coming into the West, and we must not let him go away from us without giving him some good advice." On 1 June the *Guide* urged people to write their members of Parliament expressing their views on the tariff.

The agrarian position was opposed to that of the CMA and a pitched verbal and written battle ensued. On 28 September 1910, responding to the pro-tariff position of the CMA, an editorial in the *Guide* entitled "The Manufacturers Throw Down Gauntlet" noted that the CMA was determined to press Ottawa on the tariff and it urged the farmers to counter. "It now becomes a question of manufacturers versus farmers," the *Guide* stated, claiming that "the manufacturers consider that 30,000 Western farmers have no rights whatever in the framing of the tariff." The *Guide* went on:

> This handful of 2,500 men showed their contempt for the will of the people. They declared that Canada was not a democracy and that the will of the people amounted to nothing. They boldly announced that rather than pay any attention to the people they would go to Ottawa when parliament opened and deal with the members at Ottawa. What does that mean? Simply that the manufacturers believe that their money carries more weight than the combined influence of the farmers of Canada. These manufacturers who have exacted toll from the farmers for the past generation have snapped

their fingers in the face of public opinion. They have declared their contempt for the people. They have practically said, "We are the people who control the parliament of Canada and make the tariff. We will do as we like and the farmers will pay." They make no pretense whatever that the tariff is for the benefit of the people of Canada, but acknowledged that it is merely a legalized system by which they can rob the farmers to their hearts content. What a spectacle to behold! These patriotic gentlemen whose love for country is so great, solemnly declared that the people of Canada must pay toll to them. It recalls the days of feudalism, when all the serfs and tenants lived in poverty that their over-lords might wax rich and become exceeding patriotic.

In the midst of the Canada-United States trade negotiations a major delegation of farmers converged in the "Siege of Ottawa." The idea of a major trek to Ottawa by the organized farmers had been suggested in the *Guide* as early as August. After the CMA's annual meeting in Vancouver, the *Guide* again raised the issue and by late October organizational efforts on behalf of the various farm groups were underway. Throughout the months of November and December the matter was discussed and a major position paper, referred to by the *Guide* as the "Farmers' Bill of Rights" was prepared. The role of a mass delegation was further enhanced, in the opinion of the organized farmers, by the announcement in Ottawa later in November that a tariff commission would be established. The farmers argued that this was a delaying tactic, and therefore the trek was more necessary than ever.

The Canadian Council of Agriculture was a major organizational force behind the 16 December march. The delegates met in Ottawa on 15 December to discuss issues of concern to all Canadian farmers, as there were representatives from all provinces except British Columbia. At this meeting a series of resolutions, known as the "Farmers' Platform," was passed — the first explicit declaration of concerns of the movement at the time. The first resolution dealt with the tariff. The delegation, estimated at from 850-1,000 with 500-600 of these from the West, marched to the House of Commons on 16 December. In an unusual move the delegation was permitted to enter the House of Commons and present its various briefs and resolutions to the government.

Laurier responded cautiously to the demands of the delegation, noting a tendency for the western farmers to be more radical than their eastern counterparts. On the issue of the Hudson Bay Railway and government operation and ownership of the terminals, Laurier was equivocal. As for the tariff, he was equally vague, noting that better trade relations with the United States were important, as was the British preference. Regarding the farmers' demands for reductions in the tariffs on manufactured

51

goods, Laurier was even more vague, noting that it was a particularly difficult matter.

While there is no record of the role he played, Partridge was one of the delegates from the West. The visit to Ottawa in 1910 followed a visit Partridge had made to the capital in 1909 as part of a grain growers' delegation that was lobbying the federal government over ownership of terminal elevators. The *Canadian Annual Review* of 1910 also reports that he addressed the Canadian Clubs in Toronto and Ottawa on the issue of problems facing farmers, though no details of what he said have survived.

Amid this general debate and controversy over the tariff, a trade agreement between the United States and Canada was completed. On 21 January 1911, the agreement was announced. The organized farmers supported the agreement and the *Guide* presented their sentiments. On 26 April 1911, the *Guide* launched a vigorous attack on the opponents of the agreement, stating that the backers of the opposition were capitalists who simply wanted to use the tariff to increase prices and their profits. The agreement was characterized as a victory for the people and a blow to special privileges. The *Guide* had regularly reported on the events in Ottawa as the issue was discussed. Articles, such as one entitled "Tariff is Class Legislation," were regularly run throughout the period.

Amid the debate and agitation Borden, the Leader of the Opposition, and a leader of the anti-reciprocity forces, decided to tour the West. The *Guide* welcomed the event. The 7 June issue noted the visit on the cover, and it urged the organized farmers to meet Borden and press the same demands they had presented to Laurier the year before. Borden visited Regina on 22 June and was met by over 2,000 people at a rally. Several resolutions were presented to Borden.

As the debate over the proposed agreement raged across the nation, the Laurier administration decided to accept the Conservative challenge to make the issue the basis of an election campaign. On 29 July Parliament was dissolved and an election called for 21 September.

The Liberals concentrated their campaign on the trade agreement and the benefits that would accrue from it, while the Conservatives, particularly in the West, attempted to introduce other issues such as the railway to Hudson Bay. The *Guide* viewed the election as a contest of fundamental importance with the outcome deciding whether the vested interests of the CMA and the banks would rule over the will of the people. A cartoon in the 6 September issue of the *Guide* pictured Laurier guiding the ship of Canada toward reciprocity while the CMA and others tried to lure him onto the rocks of anti-reciprocity.

The election resulted in a substantial victory for the Conservatives, who won 132 Commons seats compared to 86 for the Liberals. Despite this margin in the House of Commons, the Conservatives only polled 3 percent more of the popular vote, receiving 51 percent compared to the Liberal's 48 percent. The national figures hide the important regional division on the issue. In Ontario, for example, the Conservatives received 57 percent of the popular vote compared to 43 percent for the Liberals while in Saskatchewan the figures were nearly reversed, the Liberals receiving 58 percent of the popular vote compared to 42 percent for the Conservatives.

The Conservatives made good on their election promise with regard to the tariff and the Reciprocity Treaty was not implemented. The Liberals also learned a lesson and it would be well over a decade before they would suggest even modest tariff revisions. For many western farmers the key lesson related to the nature of the existing political process. As neither major party seemed willing to implement tariff reforms, the call for a political party which would represent agrarian and western concerns was to grow louder in subsequent years.

The Rise of the Progressive Party

The outbreak of World War I brought about a temporary lapse in agrarian agitation and a period of economic expansion, though concern with the costs of the tariff remained important to farmers. Though the level of agrarian agitation declined, the CCA felt it was necessary to restate the farmers' key grievances. To this end the CCA republished a revised and expanded edition of the "Farmers' Platform" of 1910 which had emerged as a result of the "Siege of Ottawa." In December 1916, a new "Farmers' Platform" was released by the CCA. For some candidates it became an election platform, even though the election was not to be run along party lines in the West.

There was solid support for candidates who ran under a Unionist label in the 1917 election, and consequently there were representatives of the agrarian community in the subsequent Union government. T.A. Crerar and Henry Wise Wood were given an opportunity to be involved in the key operations of the government by being named to the cabinet; Crerar was given the position of Minister of Agriculture in the new government. For the year following the election the nation concentrated on the war effort, but as it became apparent that the Allies were winning, and as the problems in the West became worse, the unrest that the war had postponed began to emerge once more. W.L. Morton (1950: 62) summarizes these developments:

> The West had put aside its particular views in 1917, but with no intention that they should be forgotten or not brought up for review at the earliest possible moment. The drive for the reduction of the

53

tariff missed no more than a single stride because of the crisis of 1917. In the late summer of 1918 the Canadian Council of Agriculture resumed the campaign...

In November 1918 the CCA again re-issued the "Farmers' Platform," which soon came to be called the "New National Policy." Western farmers were agitating increasingly for tariff reform, particularly on the western Unionist members of Parliament. By April 1919 this pressure had become so strong that an attempt was made by the western Unionists "to find ways and means of meeting the wishes of their constituents while remaining supporters of the government" (Morton, 1950: 67). They decided to create a separate caucus of western Unionists to work within the Union government to achieve the measures which the agrarian community was demanding in the "New National Policy."

This action was not enough to cause any major shift in government policy, particularly as it related to the tariff, and the budget the Union government brought down in June 1919 proved to be unacceptable to the western members. So strong was their opposition to the budget that Crerar resigned from the cabinet and nine Union members from the West voted against the government of which they were a part. These members subsequently left the party, and since they did not feel comfortable joining the Liberals they initiated action that was to lead to the formation of a new party.

The existence in Parliament of a separate caucus of western members encouraged some agrarians to become directly involved in political action. In November 1919, the Canadian Council of Agriculture passed a resolution calling for a conference of those who would be interested in "electing supporters of the national policy to the Dominion parliament" (Morton, 1950: 94). The conference was held in Winnipeg in January 1920, and was attended by representatives of most agrarian organizations and the western members of Parliament who had left the Union party.

On 26 February 1920, the western Unionists formally constituted themselves as the National Progressive Party. This marked the official formation of the national political party many agrarians had sought since before the war. In December 1920, the CCA accepted the Progressives as the exponents of the new National Policy and recommended that all of its member provincial organizations do the same. The provincial associations subsequently did so and the party was set for the next election.

It was under the umbrella of this agrarian support that the Progressive Party entered the 1921 federal election. There were internal problems, as the party was basically divided into two factions, one represented by Crerar and his goal of a reformed Liberal Party, and the other represented by Wood, who believed that a party should be avoided that the

Progressives should be representatives of the agrarian community. These fundamental differences were not reconciled before the election, and they ultimately were to become a factor in the dissolution of the party. In the 1921 election, the Progressive candidates lived up to their mandate of representing the farmers through a campaign based on the "New National Policy."

The issue which had initially precipitated the formation of the Progressive Party had been the tariff, so this was a central issue in the party's election platform. As well as the tariff, there were demands urging the government to initiate various tax reform measures, and to assist in the demobilization of the armed forces to avoid a flood of manpower onto the labour market. There were demands for electoral reforms which would have seen reform of the Senate, the abolition of titles in Canada, and the establishment of several measures of direct legislation. Finally, there were demands for the immediate removal of the censorship which had been imposed during the war.

Despite his statements earlier regarding his disinterest in party politics, Partridge was involved in the 1921 election. A number of his friends convinced him to contest the Progressive nomination in the Wolseley constituency. He became distressed at the nominating convention when the rules committee announced that each candidate would only have five minutes to speak. Partridge spent his time denouncing the undemocratic nature of the meeting and still lost the nomination by only twelve votes.

The success of the Progressive Party in the election was unprecedented. When the ballots had been counted the party held sixty-five seats and was in a position to become the official opposition in the new Parliament. The Progressive sweep of Saskatchewan was complete:

> In the federal election of 1921 the Progressives elected 65 members of Parliament out of a total of 245 in the House of Commons. Of these, 39 were from the [west]... The only seat that was lost by the Progressives in Saskatchewan was the urban seat of Regina. The Party succeeded in polling 62.6 per cent of the total vote in the 13 predominantly rural seats of Saskatchewan. (Lipset, 1971: 79)

The fate of the Progressives in the following session and in subsequent elections has been documented elsewhere, and it is not of concern here. What is of importance is the fact that in the period following the war the agrarian population of the West did attempt to implement its platform through a distinct political movement. The dissolution of the Progressives in the House of Commons and in subsequent elections does not alter the fact that at one time the majority of the voters in Saskatchewan solidly backed a national political party which campaigned on agrarian issues.

This, then, represents the general tenor of the political climate which

E.A. Partrige and other western farmers experienced between the turn of the century and the 1920s. In terms of their efforts to impact the tariff in any substantial way, by the 1920s the agrarian community had experienced two decades of unsuccessful political activity. Despite their best efforts to impact the existing parties, and systematic efforts to seek a remedy through their own political party, there was little to be optimistic about in terms of the ability of the agrarian community to achieve lower tariffs in the face of opposition by the industrial and financial sectors. Some, such as Partridge, clearly began to rethink the nature of the polity and political power in Canada. As we shall see, Partridge's subsequent musings on the issue of political power were to lead to some surprising conclusions.

Epilogue: The Making of a Radical

We have virtually no information on the details of Partridge's life during the World War I period, though it is clear that a series of personal tragedies and the broader economic, social and political processes we have been describing had a profound impact on him and his understanding of the world. In the period preceding the war Partridge was beginning to develop a more radical analysis of the class structures of his society and the associated relations of power and domination. We also know that by the 1920s, when he laid out a systematic critique of his society and his blueprint for the future, Partridge's thinking had become much more radical in virtually every way, including his assessment of the nature of the state in capitalist society, and the possibilities of social, political and economic reform as a means of making society more democratic and equalitarian. What happened to Partridge between the prewar period and the early 1920s that so changed him?

In his book, *A War on Poverty*, Partridge alludes to a period is his life when "considerable reading and much reflection — not material possessions, but physical infirmity due to accident and loss of health" (p. 25) provided him with an opportunity to rethink his philosophy of life and what he felt had to be done in order to make the world a better and more humane place. In addition to losing his leg, Partridge and his wife suffered other personal tragedies between 1914 and 1918. On 14 June 1914 two of their daughters, Enid and May, went swimming in a slough near the farm. May, who was just 22 years old, apparently suffered cramps and drowned. Then, with the outbreak of World War I, both of their sons joined the armed forces. Harold became a member of the Royal Air Force while Charles became a member of the Princess Patricia Canadian Light Infantry. The letters the boys wrote home seem to have been family treasures, with the local paper carrying copies. Then, Charles was declared missing in action, his death apparently coming on 15 September 1916. Less than two years later, Harold was killed during a training flight in England.

Faced with these personal tragedies, it is understandable that Partridge became active in the agrarian movement. As has been noted, the war brought on a general decline in agrarian agitation, though the CCA kept the tariff issue alive though the 1917 election and into the 1920s. While there was a temporary lull in agitation, the basic structural conditions that had produced the cooperative movements and the agitation for tariff reform remained and one can argue that it was the very structures of the political economy of the Prairies that continued to radicalize Partridge as he paused to reflect.

We must keep in mind that the first three decades of this century saw truly radical change on the Canadian Prairies. Partridge understood the fact that by working collectively, the farmers of the region had challenged some of the larger corporations in the country and in the process had changed the fundamental nature of the economy of the region. He knew that by the time of the Great Depression the private grain trade had gone from a position of power and dominance to one of being a minor player, as the vast majority of farmers sold the bulk of their grain to one of the various cooperatives. Partridge had helped build a retail sector for the cooperative movement which transformed retailing in many towns and villages. For some, a strong cooperative movement was an end in itself, but Partridge began to realize that the true benefits of cooperation could only be reaped through a radical transformation of capitalist society and the establishment of a "cooperative commonwealth." He increasingly felt the need to lay out in print what his experience with the political economy of the region and his readings had taught him.

As we shall see when we consider the outcome of Partridge's reflections as manifested in his book, one of the central issues that came to occupy Partridge was the nature and role of the state in capitalist society. For many in the West, the Progressive Party was an opportunity to challenge the legitimacy and domination of two established but ideologically similar parties. Farmers and workers had been forced to organize their own political parties and had discovered that they had a great deal in common when it came to concerns about the nature of economic and political power in Canada. The inability of the existing party system to cope with some of the demands of farmers and workers had led them increasingly to question the efficacy of the British parliamentary system. Three decades of agrarian protest had had virtually no impact on federal tariff policy. As we have seen, when it came to tariff policy, at virtually every turn the manufacturing sector seemed to dominate state policy and action. For thoughtful individuals such as Partridge, there was reason to reevaluate the nature of the state in capitalist society.

In the time that Partridge and his wife were farming, the agrarian movement had transformed the social fabric of the region. The different organizations, cooperatives, associations and parties that made up the larger movement had changed the social and cultural landscape. The themes of cooperation and community unity that were advocated by many of the supporters and members of the movement had become an important part of the way in which the social infrastructure was built and operated and Partridge understood this, though he wanted to take this spirit to what, for him, was its logical conclusion.

As the 1920s drew to a close, Partridge left the Prairies forever. Again, tragedy played a role. On 30 April 1926, Mary was gardening when she suffered a fatal heart attack. A year later Partridge moved off "The Bluffs" for the last time and shortly thereafter took up residence in Victoria, British Columbia, where his youngest daughter lived. Increasingly afflicted with arthritis and lingering complications from the amputated leg, he died in 1931 — apparently a suicide — from inhaling gas in his apartment.

Before we examine some of the radical ideas that Partridge came to hold by the mid-1920s, it is important to try and draw some preliminary conclusions about how he shaped and was shaped by history and society. We know that in addition to changing the social, political, economic and cultural landscape, the agrarian movement also changed those who participated in it. The fact that over the years many westerners were willing to embrace new and often radical ideas and measures is no coincidence. Participation in a process such as the agrarian social movement clearly had an impact on these individuals. Indeed, it is possible to claim that the changes that some people experienced in terms of their individual characters and behaviours were no less radical than the changes the movement made to society. Some indication of the changes that were occurring in Partridge's thinking can be gleaned from the discussion above. However, a true measure of the impact that his participation in the movement had on him can only be understood if we examine his ideas, modes of thought, and philosophy late in his life. We can do this because he recorded his thoughts, ideas, philosophy and beliefs in a book — *A War on Poverty*.

CHAPTER 4

E.A. Partridge as Revolutionary and Visionary:

A War on Poverty

Though we lack the concrete historical data to provide a detailed account of Partridge's activities during the postwar period, we have a general idea about what was happening in his life. He had a brief association with the Progressive Party, supported the new Farmers' Union, initially supported the drive for wheat pools, continued to read and began to think through and prepare to write a book.

It seems apparent that Partridge's book, eventually completed in 1925 and entitled *A War on Poverty: The One War That Can End War*, was an opportunity to proclaim and articulate his philosophy of life, views of politics, critique of capitalist society and vision of a better world. He used the book to lay out what he felt had to be done, what he had learned in over two decades of social and political activism, and what he had come to believe as a result of his experiences. Partridge was very explicit about the book and its purpose, referring to it as "A Call to Conference." He opened it with the following words:

> An invitation to well-meaning men and women, especially those in Western Canada, *to come together in conference,* through the *medium of the printed page,* with the hope of so *elevating and clarifying our common thinking,* that *immediate* and *concerted action* for the solution of our *pressing socio-economic problems* shall follow. (p. i)

It is apparent that in order to more fully understand "that man Partridge," some detailed consideration of the central themes he addressed in *A War on Poverty* is now in order. After we have a more systematic grasp of his views on a number of issues, we will offer a way of interpreting and understanding why he came to hold them.

The Potential of Humanity and Partridge's Humanism

The betterment of mankind was central to Partridge's life. He refused to accept that the way people were or lived at any given moment was inevitable or all that they were capable of. The belief that people were capable of much more than they have exhibited throughout history was a constant theme in Partridge's thought. In 1907 he made an impassioned speech to the GGGC annual meeting in which he laid out, for the first time, an argument which was to become the basis of his entire social, economic and political philosophy — human beings have capacities and potentials beyond those they might exhibit at any particular historical moment.

The 1907 speech contained Partridge's comments about community, class, and individual duties and responsibilities. While he acknowledged that many humans were completely preoccupied with individualistic and selfish matters, he noted that "a man is capable of communistic effort and self-sacrifice." The same speech referred to those who were individualistic and selfish as "hogs." The key point in Partridge's analysis of these various "hogs" was his conclusion that these animals must not be simply scorned because "they are our brothers — children of the same Infinite Father but with their spiritual consciousness not yet sufficiently developed to recognize their relationship either to Him or to their fellow men."

The key to the development of human potential or possibilities was, for Partridge, education. By example and education, in the broadest use of the term, those not yet capable of true human conduct, as opposed to "hog conduct," "may see their defects of character in all their repulsiveness." They would then come to understand a fundamental truth of human existence:

> as you extend a helping hand to some one below you, another hand, the hand of some one above you will reach down, as it has often done before, and help *you* a little forward and upward on the eternal path of progress. Picture yourself as one in the living chain of a party of Alpine climbers and you have an illustration of the thought I wish to convey and a symbol of race consciousness.

The theme of human potential and human possibilities is an important part of Partridge's *A War on Poverty*. Indeed, it could be argued that his entire philosophy and hopes for the future were predicated on the assumption that humans were capable of much more than the behaviour they exhibited. In order to make the point, Partridge referred to Darwinian theory. He stated that he was little concerned with where or what we came from, nor with our ultimate destination in the light of our future being an endless journey. He was very interested, however, in "our transient state and the prospects of immediately, and continually hereafter, improving it." The key to improving the status of this transient state, he argued, was education. The realization of what Partridge often referred to as the "potential happiness of humanity" could only begin to be realized once humans were capable of thought, analysis and reflection — all of which are dependent on education and knowledge.

According to Partridge, humanity should not be judged by its past or current practices. Rather, other possibilities and potentials should be developed:

> Life isn't just a murky little mill-pond stocked with bullheads, carp, and suckers, prey for a few greedy pike, as our "safe and sane,"

unimaginative, hard-headed, "practical" men of affairs seem prone to think: rather, life is a boundless ocean, with illimitable possibilities of growth and change within its unfathomable depths and immeasurable breadths of being. Shakespeare saw the vision:

"There are more things in heaven and earth, Horatio,
Than are dreamt of in our philosophy." (pp. 13-14)

To accomplish this, it would be necessary to encourage the development of visions — to "encourage the seekers of universal social good to persevere in this dark hour, and silence those who speak of them as futile visionaries, and dreamers of foolish dreams that cannot possibly come true... We suffer not from visionaries, but from those who lack vision" (p. 13). Partridge's devotion to the improvement of the human species was at the core of his existence.

At the beginning of his book Partridge notes that he had discovered, as a boy, that Edward meant "Guardian of Happiness," while Alexander meant "Helper of Men." He stated that he had striven "intermittently at least, to be not unworthy of the titles bestowed on me at my christening" (p. xv). At the centre of his philosophy was what he called humanism:

I am a humanitarian. I believe that a wide-spread acceptance of the gospel of humanitarianism must precede any greatly worth-while socio-economic re-construction, since such re-construction must be the result of good-will rather than of guile or force — the sweetening of human relationships being worth much more to society than even the enlargement and evener distribution of material wealth without it! much as these are to be desired. Besides, the latter would naturally follow the former. So, I am a humanitarian. My religion, if any, is humanitarianism — a devotion to the service of Man. God can look after himself: many a man can't: as in Canaan in the First Century, so in Canada in the Twentieth, it can only too often be truthfully said: "Foxes have holes and the birds of the air have nests, but the son of man hath not where to lay his head." To those who associate "religion" with the worship of God rather than the service of man, I answer from their own text-book: "He that loveth not his brother whom he hath seen, how can he love God whom he hath not seen?" (pp. 33-34)

As noted in this passage, Partridge was convinced that the full development of humanity and human potential required a radical restructuring of the existing social, economic and political system. Partridge developed this point even more forcefully in the following comments which lead us to his more concrete analysis of the nature of the socioeconomic system he was interested in analyzing:

We poor, silly, smart-alecks, on this corner of "the footstool," like other worldly-wise fools elsewhere, are, most of us — poor, well-to-do, and rich, alike — cross-purposedly "messing about," expending our energies, largely in non-creative contendings with one another, mainly robbing and sneak-thievings — under forms of law, of course — and resistings of these in sundry ways, — equally legitimate, when no injunction issues, but not so socially distinguished — instead of deliberately, unitedly directing our co-ordinated wit, strength, and skill to the co-operative exploitation of our non-human environment of pasture, meadow, orchard, arable, forest and mineral lands, fishing waters, brute life, domestic and wild — as humanely as possible — and sources of natural power, for the quick and easy providing of all of us with the things generally regarded as necessary to physical and mental well-being; leaving the gratification of more individual tastes and desires to be secured by individual effort, or the joint effort of like-minded persons, in the ample time that might be salvaged from the hideous wastes of our present chaotic, catch-as-catch-can, dog-eat-dog, individualistic, competitive system, by replacing it with the saner method of communal co-operation. (pp. 42-43)

Capitalism as Class Exploitation and Domination

Central to Partridge's critique of capitalist society and why it was incapable of facilitating the development of human potential was the concept of class. While he may have never developed a sociologically sophisticated definition of class, the term was employed with increasing precision and in an increasingly critical manner as Partridge's thinking developed.

As early as 1904, in his address to the TGGA annual meeting, Partridge was using the term "class," referring to farming as an occupation and speaking about the need of the agricultural class to press its concerns to government. By the time he wrote his 1905 letter appealing for support for the concept of a grain-growers' grain company, he was referring to various classes, with "class" being synonymous with economic interest. By 1906, when he addressed the SGGA, Partridge was beginning to use language which recognized, in implicit terms, the existence of class conflict as opposed to the mere existence of different interests in society. Partridge referred in this regard to "those who prey alike on the toilers in the factory and on the farm." The idea of "those who toil," or "the productive classes," was to become increasingly important in his thinking.

In Partridge's 1907 speech to the GGGC, many of these emerging themes receive their first systematic exposition in an analysis that previewed his subsequent critical analysis of capitalist society. It was in this speech that he compared class, community and individual interests and duties. In terms of his class analysis, the speech marked one of the first occasions in which he publicly examined the nature of those classes that opposed and exploited the farmers. He began this aspect of his analysis by simply stating that the "capitalist classes" had long recognized the value of acting cooperatively and in unison to achieve their goals. This practice had allowed them to enhance their economic interests and make possible their control over politics and the press.

The ranks of the "capitalist classes" included financial interests such as bankers and commercial interests such as grain traders and manufacturers. Opposed to these classes were what he termed the producing classes. Although he did not explicitly define the term, he referred to various traditional categories of wage labour which had formed trade unions, and the farmers. The central purpose of the speech was to advocate the establishment of an organization that would act like a farmers' trade union.

It is again in *A War on Poverty* that we find the most explicit exposition of Partridge's thought. The book begins with "A Call to Conference," in which Partridge lays out the purpose of the treatise. He explained who he was interested in addressing:

> I especially desire the attendance of all those who now willingly live by useful labour, or would so live if they could, — their own of course: all else is beggary or thievery — intrinsically useful labour, whether of hand or brain, whether "in field or factory, mine or mart," laboratory or lecture room, engine-cab or elsewhere, that they, individually, without exception, — and as a preparation for the inclusion of them all in a co-operative organization for the easy and abundant supplying of their common needs — may be made aware of the complete community or solidarity of their political, social, and economic interests — their political interest being but the furtherance of the other two — which are the pleasant production and satisfying consumption, or use, of abundant unenvied wealth amidst agreeable social surroundings — man being by nature a social animal. Frankly I want a chance to try, under not too unfavourable circumstances, to convince a majority of our people of the desirability, and also the feasibility, of creating a Co-operative Commonwealth, — the logical goal of the "Co-operation." (p. v)

The broad categorization of those working by useful labour remained essentially the same throughout the book. Partridge referred to the distinction between the rich and the poor, the privileged and the oppressed, and so on, but his concern was clearly with the farmers and the wage workers:

> The wage-workers are largely organized into trade-unions, and many of them have heard with not inattentive ears the clarion call: "Workers of the World, unite! You have nothing to lose but your chains, and a world to gain!"

63

The dirt farmers have their associations and unions. They, too, in considerable and ever-growing numbers are coming to realize that, like the wage-workers, they have "nothing to lose but *their* chains." A suggestive motto of theirs is "Organization, Education, Co-operation," which its originator, the late Fred Green of revered memory among pioneer Saskatchewan farmers, interpreted thus: "We organize that we may educate; we educate that we may co-operate; we co-operate that we may get what we go after." (p. 160)

Partridge argued that wage labourers and farmers faced a common problem — others benefited from their productive labour. The chief outcome of the situation in which some benefit at the expense of others was the concentration of wealth and its many attendant problems. In exploring the nature of the relationship between the accumulation of wealth by some and virtual poverty for others, Partridge offered some of his most powerful prose:

Capitalism stands for monopoly of ownership in the means of production, distribution, and exchange of wealth, and consequent mastership, involving exploitation, of those who do not own. Capitalists, when not too drunken with power and the pride of possession, know that despite their *legal* title, they have no *moral* right to monopolize the *natural resources of a people, either by purchase or lease*, or other methods of securing them; they know also that as for the *artificial means for supplying the people's needs*, the disinherited ones who operate them as hired servants, have, in the mass, paid for them over and over again by the excess of their earnings over what they received in pay since starting to work for wages.

It is easy, of course, to say that Labor and the farmer get too little for their products, and that the manufacturer, etc., get too much, but we ought, if possible, to back up our statement with facts. Our facts moreover ought to be in some way substantiated. (p. 47)

Partridge presented sets of data on production costs, including wages, in major industries as compared to the profits that accrued to the companies. He noted, for example, that flour millers received over $2.4 million in profits on a payroll of about $760,000, while in the meat-packing industry in 1920, the average worker received $850 a year in wages yet produced over $6,200 in profits (p. 50). Partridge went on:

These, remember, are their own figures. They could be quoted page after page. However, I think the point has been made that the workers have produced many times over the value of the wages they have received. It is not those who grow the grain and the beef, not those who mill or kill who get the big rake-off, but those who are in control. In a word, society is divided into those who produce and do not possess, and those who possess and do not produce: of those who live without working, and those who work without living, in the large sense in which the word "Life" should be used in the Twentieth Century.

Debt-encumbered petty proprietors, preyed upon by usurers, and wage-workers dependent on private employers for opportunity to live meagerly as hired hands, are the modern equivalents of the serf and the chattel slave of an earlier age. The lot of these types by lapse of time has improved with the increase of man's control over nature, but their relation is still, in essence, that of serf to lord, slave to master, though masked and cloaked by superficial semblances of liberty, equality, and fraternity that deceive no one but the wilfully blind or the hopelessly foolish. Social science should bear finer fruit of noble living in the Twentieth Century than this. (pp. 50-51)

While the appropriation of wealth produced by the labouring or productive classes, to use Partridge's words, was one of the central causes of poverty in capitalist society, poverty itself was not the only problem manifested by the system. Partridge became increasingly concerned with the power of some classes to control politics and the state.

The State as Class Domination

Partridge's thinking concerning the nature of the state, government, and political power underwent significant change over the years. In his first comments on the nature of politics and government, he was essentially "accepting" of the prevailing institutions. In his early remarks on politics he called on farmers to enlighten governments as to the legislative needs of the agrarian community. The liberal view of the role and functions of government apparent in his early comments corresponded to the basic view of government implicit in the notion of the Partridge Plan. The Partridge Plan, as discussed earlier, was a proposal to have various levels of government take over the ownership and operation of grain elevators in order to prevent private interests from using food production and distribution for the generation of profits. The assumption was that government basically operated in the interests of all citizens and would not have a vested interest in acting in the interest of any particular class, but rather would operate the system in the interests of the entire society.

Partridge's acceptance of the basic structures of the liberal democratic state was still apparent in his 1908 call at the annual meeting of the SGGA for the voting out of office of those opposed to government ownership of elevators. He had stated in his 1907 speech to the GGGC meeting that he did not believe in party politics, but offered no elaboration.

If we pick up his thinking in this regard during the 1920s we find a radical shift. In the "A Call to Conference" section of his book, he previewed the themes he would develop as they related to the structures of the state. In outlining some of the radical changes that the book would argue for, he noted that a change in the form of state would accompany changes in economic organization:

> The fullest, most effective co-operation would seem to need to be State-wide in its application, — to involve turning the State into a co-operative society — making it a Co-operative Commonwealth...
> (p. xi)

The precise nature of the proposed new state will be discussed later, but first we must examine why Partridge felt that such a restructuring was necessary.

As we have seen, Partridge was concerned with the power that had become concentrated in the hands of the few who dominated economic life. Those with economic power had been able, Partridge maintained, to control the state and establish laws that benefited them:

> Force and chicanery characterize all systems of law and government, past and present. Laws are made in the special interest of the makers, or, shall we say, the manufacturers — those who own the busy law factories we call legislatures: governments are operated for the benefit of the governors — the land lords and money lords, the lords of the machine, of the road, and of the market-place — and sometimes a war lord — who, with their retainers, subsist as did the more picturesque plunderers of an earlier and more frankly brutal age. There are not now, and never have been, countries where the poor — far and away the most numerous in any population — have had, or now have, any considerable say in the making or enforcing of the laws — if we except Russia where rich and poor alike, so far, seem to have made, or left things, decidedly uncomfortable for most. So, up to date, no one can say how much better or worse the rule of the poor would be than the rule of the rich — and I for one am not anxious to experiment with a view to finding out. I am for turning both the rich and the poor into the well-to-do, and having these govern themselves, so that for the first time in the history of the world, government might be in the interest of the governed. (p. 32)

Elsewhere he made the same point in somewhat different language:

> They [capitalists] have taken to heart the old Roman maxim of government — "Divide and rule." Knowing that the perpetuation of their Order lies in preserving the unjust laws relating to property, and that these can be kept unchanged only by keeping the mass of citizens too ignorant to challenge them, and then combine to alter them through concerted political action, they conspire to keep control of both the means of legislation and of education. (p. 51)

In several passages Partridge poured out his disapproval of the manner by which politics in Canada operated:

And the Barons of this new-old Noble Order of Chivalry are still in the saddle: their slaves still sweat in mines and workshops in the East and their serfs still till the soil in the West: their hirelings in the two-chambered federal parliament and in the nine dinky sub-parliaments, belching patriotism, still go through the solemn farce of pretending to pass laws in the interest of the Common People. (p. 56)

Later in the book, he elaborated on this theme:

In the typical State, to-day, — though something better is aborning — individuals profit or are penalized by their inclusion in it according as they belong to dominant or subordinate groups. Gumplivicz and Oppenheimer agree (I quote from H.E. Barnes) that "the State is fundamentally made up of a number of conflicting groups and classes, each with its special interest" which, "instead of operating as a conciliating and harmonizing agent, furnishes the authoritative political means of allowing a minority to rule and carry on the economic exploitation of the majority."

Party politics is a "confidence game," highly amusing, no doubt, as well as profitable to the operators who employ it to gain their sinister end — the betrayal of the public interest for private gain. It is a device by which the potentially all-powerful people, divided into two or more contending armies of voters, are induced to engage in furious battles over questions of small or no economic significance, leaving the real causes of their general lack of comfort and well-being unattacked, often unsuspected. Even political parties (I again quote Professor Barnes to support my contention) are no longer looked upon as "unselfish philanthropic organizations devoted to advancing the interests of the country as a whole, but as organizations centering about a set of distinct interests for which they desire to obtain public recognition, aid and protection. (pp. 110-11)

Partridge felt the solution to the situation was at hand — a radical restructuring of the entire fabric of Canadian society. It was to promote this restructuring that he wrote his book.

Partridge's Utopian Vision

Partridge has frequently been referred to as a visionary, and indeed he saw himself as one in his book. *A War on Poverty* contains fascinating detail of the outlines of Partridge's prospective new society for Canada:

COALSAMAO

Coalsamao (pronounced Co-al'-sa-ma"-o) gets its name from the first two letters of the names of the former provinces now merged to form it (Br.) Columbia, Alberta, Saskatchewan, Manitoba, with the final "o" for that part of Ontario also included.

It is a fully self-governed, self-constituted State with a single one-chambered legislative and administrative body, corresponding to a House of Representatives, but called "The High Court of Control," consisting of twenty-five members elected annually, sitting in perpetual session, during their term of office, chiefly for investigatory, supervisory, and administrative purposes, there being but little legislative work for them to do.

This High Court of Control carries on under the terms of a written Constitution, changes in which can be initiated only by concerted action of at least a fourth of the primary organized socio-economic units called "Camps," and consummated by popular assent indicated by a favorable plebiscite.

The Constitution defines "The State of Coalsamao" as a "Co-operative Commonwealth" — "an association of the inhabitants thereof for the effective employment of the combined strength of the bodies, brains, and belongings of the associates, for the securing of their common safety from the attacks of external and internal foes, human and non-human; for the adequate and easy supplying of their common needs and the effective advancement of their common interests as recognized by the majority; and also, for the extending of timely help and protection to such of them as in sudden vicissitude shall have need of help and protection." (pp. 130-31)

Coalsamao was to be a distinctly decentralized society, organized around local units which Partridge referred to as "camps." Each "camp" was to have a population of between 3,000 and 7,000 and was to be systematically organized to ensure that all the necessary production, transportation and exchange were carried out. Each "camp" would be self-governing and would elect delegates to a "regional rally" or "assembly." The "regional assembly" would in turn elect the members of the "high court." Partridge described the nature of the "high court":

The High Court is centrally located and has radio-communication with each camp, and such of the field forces, as are not working under local direction, as of a camp or a number of camps co-operating for the accomplishment of some purpose of less than national import. The "Court" is in perpetual session under a presiding officer selected from its membership and styled High Chief. Members may not absent themselves for more than thirty days without rendering their office vacant except when officially employed elsewhere by direction of the Court. Seats rendered vacant are filled by the Court by choosing the "alternate" if possible, if not then the "runner-up" if there be one, otherwise some other member of the Regional Assembly to which the former member belonged. The High Court carries on its chief activities under ten Departments of State:

1. Administration and Control.

2. Order and Justice.
3. Education and Publicity.
4. Health and Well-being.
5. Communication and Transport.
6. Production and Employment.
7. Distribution and Exchange.
8. Public Works and Services.
9. Research and Inventions.
10. International Relations. (p. 133)

Since Coalsamao was to be organized as a "co-operative common-wealth," its economic system was to involve public or social ownership:

> an association for the co-operative carrying-on of their every-day affairs — the production and distribution among them of a sufficiency of food, clothing, shelter, furnishings, fuel, and what not, to meet their common needs; the reproduction and proper increase of the communally-owned working capital and reserves, besides the necessary public buildings, in addition to schools and workshops, tools, machinery, and transport facilities; the rearing and education of their young, provision for the comfort of the aged and disabled, and full, free, and immediate medical and surgical care for all. (pp. 134-35)

Partridge envisioned a radically different form of society:

> For the first time in history had a State so ordered its affairs that there was complete community of interest among its citizens. Its motto, and its practice also, now, was, "Each for all and all for each." Human nature had not materially altered, as it were, over-night; but the viewpoint of a large number of the people in Coalsamao — their conception of what sort of conduct was in their best interest — undoubtedly had. This was due to a sudden and wide promulgation and as sudden and wide an acceptance — the time of propaganda and the psychological moment having for once happily coincided — of the new-old, sociological discovery of the absolute solidarity of human interest on the higher level of living, the truth that "the happiness of each is dependent upon the happiness of all." (p. 135)

The transition to the new society would, Partridge argued, be without violence:

> I believe there is enough of this divine discontent, social spirit, sympathy, love of justice, and idealism among us to-day, that, reinforced by moral impulses and intellectual powers now dormant in the mass of citizenry for lack of education, would make the creation of a happy social organization possible in a few short years, without violence, and with a practically painless transition from the state of things we complain of, to the state of things many people sigh for, but do nothing to bring into being. (pp. 23-24)

A restructuring as radical as that proposed, however, would have dis-locations and disruptions — these, Partridge argued, were unavoidable. The key to the future must be a radical break with the past:

So thought the founders of Coalsamao. They might have voiced their conclusions thus: "In reconstituting a Society which in its origins, its expansions, and its continuing activities, reeks of "rights" founded on wrongs, "justice" established on injustice, "moral sanctions" which are merely fraud's endorsement of the behavior of crooked force, we cannot hope in a majority of cases to make unchallenged adjustments of reward to desert: then why try? We had far better *make a clean sweep, and get a fresh start.* We will see to it that everyone now, and from now on, shall have little cause to complain of wilful trespass on his or her right to enjoy life, being worthy to do so. We must extinguish some of the "rights" that are founded on wrongs, such as the "right" to individual property as contrasted with communal use-possession, in land, the "right" to enforce private contracts, as agreements to pay rent and interest made in ignorance or under compulsion of need; and we must put an end to sundry law-supported privileges that make life too easy for some and too hard for others. But we will extend the protection of the State to those expropriated wherever the circumstances make it necessary or becoming from a humanitarian standpoint. A pension in lieu of the property taken, or the privilege withdrawn, will soothe the sorrows, break the fall, of the dispossessed incumbents, and as for the descendants of such, they will not miss something they never had. We will pension the ex-propertied. We, who worked, were obliged to keep them under the Old System, sometimes much too well, and with much difficulty because of the various handicaps inherent in that system. It will be easier done by pensioning the lot, and each death will lessen the load. (pp. 137-38)

In Coalsamao there would be fewer laws, rules and regulations. How-ever, one essential principle would prevail:

In Coalsamao there are very few laws: so few, and so simple and understandable, are they, having so little to do with monetary and proprietary interests, that the citizens are neither afflicted with lawsuits nor burdened with the maintenance of lawyers. In other countries most laws have to do with "real" property and with contracts of one sort or another, the outcome of private ownership of "real" property. Here there is no private ownership of such things as mines, timber-limits, farm lands, industrial and business sites, residential locations, water-fronts or rights of way, nor of large-scale "businesses" which come from private ownership of such, consequently no leasings, sellings or bequeathings of these. There are no contracts between citizens enforceable by law, nor obligations with which the law has anything to do, if we except the mutual natural obligations of man and wife, parent and child, citizen and fellow-citizen, that have to do with decent behavior and which are pretty well embodied in the Ten Commandments, which that celebrated dictator named Moses compiled and endeavoured to buttress with a higher authority than his own. For instance, there is no provision in Coalsamao's laws for the collection of rent, or interest, or recovery of a loan, or for redemption of a promise, whether dischargeable in services, in money, or in kind; but there are laws designed for the discouragement of offences against the dignity, liberty, mental and moral integrity, and person of all citizens, and others for securing to them the peaceful possession and free enjoyment of personal property. The State takes upon itself the obligation of defending its citizens against wrongs suffered at the hands of their fellows. (pp. 138-39)

While there are more details available in Partridge's book, these passages serve to illustrate the extent to which Partridge was not only a social critic, but a utopian visionary as well. The essential point is that it was his role as social critic that led him to make propositions concerning the need to radically restructure society.

On Building Socialism

The proposals for the establishment of Coalsamao were developed during the early 1920s and presented in *A War on Poverty*. As the decade ended Partridge moved away from this particular project, as he became more interested in seeing a union of the forces of labour and farmers. Evidence gathered by the UGG in the process of preparing a commemoration to Partridge indicated that he was a devoted reader of *The Furrow* during the late 1920s. *The Furrow* was the official organ of the Progressive Farmers' Education League and its successor, the Farmers' Unity League. Both of these organizations were intimately connected with the Communist Party of Canada. Correspondence exists between Partridge and representatives of the Farmers' Unity League expressing agreement on several points.

Near the end of his life Partridge turned to the advocacy of political projects which were more in line with the trends apparent in his day. As Honourary President of the UFC, Partridge sent a letter to be read at the 1931 convention. In the letter, he argued for an alliance of the wealth producers of the society and for united political action:

The proposed alliance to secure the election of a workers' government to replace the owners' government we now have should be as popular with our penniless, marketless farmers as with propertyless, jobless wage-workers. Could our farmers' union, under the present circumstances, do better than to transform itself into an enlarged "Educational League," and a propaganda-

71

spreading and recruiting agency for the proposed non-vocational union that seems to be the next logical step towards economic freedom for those who toil, wherever they toil. The typical prairie farmer today, in reality is neither an owner of property nor an employer of wage-workers and has all to gain and nothing to lose by the transition from an owners' to a workers' government and from a system of production for profit to a system of production for use since there is no longer any profit in any sort of farming except the sort "Big Business" engages in — "the farming of the farmers."

A workers' (wealth producers') government, as contrasted with an owners' (wealth accumulators') government, would hold views and take positions in sharp contrast with those commonly held and taken by the only kind of government Canadians at the time had ever lived under. "Russia," Partridge argued, "furnishes the only present-day example of a workingman's government but a capitalist-controlled press leaves our people uninformed, when not misinformed, as to what is really being accomplished socially and economically over there."

Partridge went on to state that such a workers' government would instigate a broad policy of public ownership, including factories and farms. This last point brings us to the issue of economic organization, also of keen importance to Partridge:

> A workers' government, giving the phrase its broadest interpretation, would take the side of public ownership, of all natural means of wealth-production. It would favour public ownership, not only of all natural means of wealth-production, but it would also favour public ownership of many of the more important artificial means of production, distribution and exchange and in some cases their operation as public utilities for mutual protection of producers and consumers from the effect of individualistic greed where private ownership and operation afford opportunities for exploitation, which is a polite expression that means *thieving under forms of law*.

> It would quite possibly solve the problem of the unemployed or underpaid wage-workers and dispossessed and unequipped farmers by making them civil servants in the Department of Public Works, that is to say, hiring them at fair wages to work in State-owned-and-operated factories and farms and elsewhere, where the raw materials of wealth production were being secured by human efforts for the supplying of human need and the satisfying of human desire.

Beyond Cooperatives

Throughout his life, Partridge developed an ever more radical and critical appraisal of capitalist society. In terms of his concern with the nature of economic life in society, he exhibited a hostility to unrestrained private ownership of society's productive apparatuses. As has been noted, his early writings and speeches contained many references to the problems Partridge felt were associated with private ownership of the railways, industry and banking.

In his later life Partridge refined these early concerns into a more systematic critique of the structures of capitalist economic organization. Indeed, a central thesis of *A War on Poverty* is that there is an intimate connection between poverty and private ownership of society's productive capabilities. Partridge noted that it "fails to indicate the root cause of most of our politico-socio-economic ills in the vicious laws relating to *privilege* and to *certain forms of property*" (p. 58). He saw the central problem of capitalist society as the fact that its productive energies were oriented around production for profit and not for use (p. 45). The private ownership of society's productive resources and their utilization in the interests of the generation of profit for those who own them led to the concentration of wealth in the hands of a few. Most of society's problems arose from this concentration:

> The immediate cause of our present plight is the intolerable, pushed-to-the-limit exploitation of the poor, the weak, the unfortunate, the uninstructed, and the simple, by the rich, the strong, the fortunate, the instructed and the cunning through various forms of opportunity — of the more scrupulous by the less so, as well. Concentration of wealth and opportunity in the hands of the few is the logical consequence of the present predaceous competitive system consistently and persistently pursued. Where the means of production, the stores of manufactured goods, and the money are all in the same hands "business as usual" is impossible. And that is the condition the Capitalist-Competitive System has already brought us near to, and which may be characterized as capitalistic slavery as contrasted with chattel slavery. Excessive accumulation of means on the one side, and the consequent almost complete lack of means on the other and vastly more populous side, has resulted in a sort of financial, industrial and commercial impasse or stale-mate, that promises to put an end to the game of Beggar-My-Neighbour that has so absorbed the players, big and little, on the but lately utilized "Great Chess Board" with its millions of green and black squares, "out where the West begins." (pp. 89-90)

The solution to the problems generated by the economic structures of capitalism were to be found in the transformation of those structures. This transformation would provide the necessary preconditions for the abolition of the problems associated with monopoly and private ownership. As we have seen, in some of his prewar writing Partridge argued that many of the problems inherent in the competitive nature of capitalism could be

73

remedied through the establishment of groups which would look after the interests of their members. Farmers' cooperatives, for example, would counter the weight and power of the organized grain trade and manufacturers. As the years passed, his criticisms of capitalism became more and more radical. By the 1920s he took a position decidedly hostile to the argument that maintained that all farmers and workers needed to do was offset the power of capital by organizing themselves. This was, of course, the position that he himself had advocated in 1905, but by 1926 he recognized that such a proposition did not go far enough. Actions such as the formation of a farmers' cooperative merely substituted one form of competition for another:

> "Let the buyer beware!" says the old adage: "Let the seller beware!" say I. There can be no peace between buyer and seller, as such. Only when both are merged in the same co-operative group, to produce identity of interest, can social solidarity and peace and plenty for all be achieved, which is true co-operation's worth-while goal. All short of this is *group competition* — commercial war, or subjugation for one group and a mean triumph for the other.

> Permit a parenthetical reference to the "Wheat Pool." Suppose the "Pool" put up the price of wheat to a permanently higher level, actual and relative, what good would it do the landless farmer's son who wanted to follow his father's occupation. The gain would accrue to the land owner, who, capitalizing the gain in an enhanced purchase price to the prospective buyer, would leave the farmer of the new generation no better off than the usury-robbed farmer of this.

> We seek relief in the multiplication of our organizations and our laws, rather than in the development of character. We are smothered under an ever-growing mountain of law-supported obligations and of prohibitive legislation. "The more corrupt the State, the more laws; the more laws, the more lawlessness," as the history of Prohibition here and elsewhere, exemplifies. (pp. 106-7)

Partridge left a fragment of a poem in his handwriting which dealt with the formation of the wheat pool:

> The Wheat Pool

> The farmers jumped into a "pool."
> What was their aim I wonder?
> To get a fair price for their wheat?
> Or organize plunder?

Although the poem was unfinished, it illustrated the dramatic evolution of his thinking and the radical nature of his critique of capitalist society.

Partridge on Religion

The last aspect of Partridge's thought to be examined here is his views

74

on religion and God. It can be argued that one's views on these matters are a central part of one's overall philosophy, and this was certainly the case with Partridge.

In the 1907 speech to the GGGC, Partridge used the phrase "children of the same Infinite Father" when referring to humans. This sort of reference was common in his early writings and speeches and *A War on Poverty* was ripe with references to God. The Deity referred to, however, was clearly related to the social and political analysis that Partridge was developing.

In the "A Call to Conference" section which opens his book, Partridge challenged Christians:

> Quite a large percentage of our population, men and women, I am led to believe, repeat what is known as "The Lord's Prayer," daily. It seems a silly thing to pray every morning for the Kingdom of Heaven to come, and not be expecting it, and, what is more, working for it. To work for a state or condition one must have some sort of a mental picture of it. To me the Kingdom of Heaven suggests a Co-operative Commonwealth. I have no desire to take it by violence, being content to help bring it in by spreading a conviction of its desirability, and the practicability of its establishment, among my fellows by means of the printed. (p. xi)

Partridge explicitly discussed the evolution and development of his beliefs and faith as they related to religious matters. He explained that he found it difficult to accept the God that Western peoples seemed to worship because this was a God "fuller of commands than compunctions; fuller of pride than pity; fuller of kingly arrogance that fatherly affection" (p. 8). Thus he explained that:

> when it came my turn to wrestle with the problems of life, I found myself unable, after a little reflection, to regard as a reality the "Good God" of my fathers, whose hideous instructions to his favored people as to their treatment of worshippers of other gods, his acts of hate-inspired violence directed against the work of his own hands, and his threat of post-mortem vengeance on unbelievers, were supposedly recorded in the "Good Book." The story of his sayings and doings, when thoughtfully read, first outraged my sense of what was fitting in a *man*, let alone a *God*, — I could not *respect*, much less *love* the personality thus portrayed — they also strained my credulity beyond the breaking point. I said to myself: "This is no portrait of a God in action: to believe in such, were it possible, would be to become a victim of despair: better to believe in nothing than to believe in such a monster." (pp. 8-9)

As a result Partridge began to regard himself as an atheist. In time, however, he again changed his views, this time inspired by teachings of and about Christ:

Contrasting the vengefulness of Jehovah with the beneficence of the man of Nazareth I turned for comfort to the reputed words of his Gospel of "Peace on earth, Good-Will towards Men," — would that this Gospel had been accepted by humanity before the last war had been fought — and his Epitome of Social Science which contains but one sentence — "Do unto others as ye would that they should do unto you." (p. 9)

Still, for Partridge, acceptance of the teachings of Christ was not the end of his spiritual search. He argued that the acceptance of the relevance of the teachings and works of Christ did not necessarily imply acceptance of the traditional Christian view of God. A deep and profound thinker, Partridge could not leave the issue alone:

Still, "a watch predicates a watch maker"; I, and the world I lived in called for a creator: so, before long, I found myself, vaguely and intermittently, it is true, and with no manner of filial affection or gratitude, believing in a Supreme Being, a Creator and Moral Governor of the Universe, "a force, not of ourselves, that" (presumably) "makes for righteousness," whose will I wanted to discover, whose wish I sought to anticipate, if only to smooth and shorten the road I must travel in the accomplishment of the purpose for which I was created — no trifling one in itself, or in its consequence for me, my reason, or what I took to be "reason," assured me — there wouldn't be all this pother, and pain for the creature as well, with futility at the end. Finally I came to feel strongly that there was too much power, and knowledge, and system, and sequence, apparent in the phenomena all around us to allow me to doubt that it was associated with the highest kind of wisdom — right-wiseness, *righteousness*; in short I developed *Faith*. (p. 10)

Partridge's ultimate acceptance of the reality of a God as "an all wise creator" led, ironically, to a commitment to an even deeper humanism. This led, in turn, to a synthesis of the various strands of his life:

To those who associate "religion" with the worship of God rather than the service of man, I answer from their own text-book: "He that loveth not his brother whom he hath seen, how can he love God whom he hath not seen?" I would see *men* put before *money*, *people* before *property*, in the handling of the world's business. It is high time for one of God's *fools* to appear on the scene and do what "the worldly-wise" declare to be impossible — *start a successful crusade for the abolition of poverty*, as being not a God-sent curse, but a man-occasioned calamity. Some fool who will attempt to effect a realization of the vision of the Carpenter of Nazareth: "Thy Kingdom come, *on Earth*." The "impossible" is always being done in the realm of physical science; why not in the region of social science?

76

I am a big enough fool for what I believe to be "righteousness' sake" to be willing to attempt it. (p. 34)

Partridge then called on professed Christians to put their principles into practice:

I adjure by the Christ you profess to follow, to go out and *work* for the coming of the Kingdom as well as *pray* for it! Your Great Exemplar cast the money changers out of the Temple, — the seat of political authority in a so-called theocracy — that it might no longer be a den of thieves. You should try to have the Houses of Parliament — the seats of political authority in this so-called democracy — ridden of thieves also. Your Teacher said: "Call no man Master." Should you then not seek to change the present industrial system, with its relation of master and servant, and the present financial system with its loaning on usury, wherein "the borrower is servant to the lender"? (p. 164)

Partridge took the point even further, challenging those who professed to follow Christ to consider the path He would have taken had He been alive in the 1920s:

Had Jesus been born nineteen hundred years later, and in Western Canada, how would He have conducted himself under present circumstances? Would He, metaphorically speaking, have been using His whip of small cords on Communists? Or on Capitalists? What think you, my Christian Friends?

"And they continued steadfastly in the apostle's doctrine and fellowship, and in breaking of bread, and in prayers.

"And fear came upon every soul: and many wonders and signs were done by the apostles.

"And all that believed were together, and had all things in common;

"And sold their possessions and goods, and parted them to all men, as every man had need." Acts 2:42-45. (p. 165)

Perhaps the most interesting aspect of Partridge's views with regard to what we are loosely calling religion was his acceptance of the concept of reincarnation. While it is clear that he accepted the possibility of reincarnation, his use of the belief had a decidedly pragmatic side, given his announced philosophic and practical humanism:

Believing in reincarnation, one would never reach the age or station in life where one would cease to be keenly interested in all efforts to make mankind universally stronger, braver, wiser, fairer, finer, kinder — free-er, too, of the foolishness of nationalism by being made aware that "In the gain or loss of one race all the rest have equal claim." Under the stimulus of such a faith there would, I think, be few among the energetic Western peoples who would not vigorously strive from early youth to extreme old age to make the world a place of universal peace, plenty, and unending progress, in the art of noble living...

Before leaving this vital subject of reincarnation, I would like in some way to support the plausibility of my appeal for at least non-rejection of the gospel of reincarnation which promises such good support to those who want to get every one interested in making the world a better and better place in which to sojourn. (pp. 28-29)

CHAPTER 5

E.A. Partridge as Intellectual

E.A. Partridge was part of an historic process — the settlement of the Canadian West and the development of the western Canadian agrarian movement. As such, he was fundamentally altered by the experiences and struggles of members of his class. As a settler he experienced, first-hand, the sting of the tariff when he purchased farm supplies and agricultural inputs. When he tried to sell his grain, he experienced the frustration of lost income because of excessive dockage, price systems he could not understand, and the failure of the transportation system. Later, as a social activist, he saw the power of the Canadian Manufacturers Association to influence tariffs while the farmers' demands went unheeded. On visiting Ottawa and Toronto he saw physical manifestations of the massive wealth he had read of in corporate reports. Even after watching his peers support the Progressive Party *en masse*, he was not able to see any significant change in the tariff policies that most western Canadians agreed worked against their interests. The state, in his experience, was not a neutral arbitrator of social conflict, but rather was part of a system of class exploitation, rule and domination.

Partridge became a social activist, an economic and political reformer, and an advocate of cooperative economic organizations. These activities seem to have changed him, as he later came to believe that as long as the basic structures and relations of the class system called capitalism remained unchanged, cooperative activity and cooperatives themselves were of no real benefit. Though various cooperatives might allow some farmers to increase their income, in terms of the larger issue of the betterment of the majority, Partridge believed they were ineffectual. Eventually Partridge came to argue that what was needed was a radical social, economic and political transformation of all aspects of the system.

Partridge and his wife experienced firsthand the devastation of war, losing both their sons. The fact that many industrial capitalists made fortunes during the war did not escape Partridge, and explains his bitter denunciation of war and profiteering. Partridge saw regional underdevelopment in Canada and the associated poverty as a real, yet artificial problem created by the fact that he lived in a capitalist society that was not capable of developing all the potential wealth in the West.

When we consider the life and times of E.A. Partridge, it is clear that he was radically changed and altered by the world around him — by what he saw and what he experienced. Yet, other members of his class shared these experiences but did not develop the kind of radical under-standing he did, nor did they share his vision of a better world. An important question that emerges is why did Partridge follow the course of political and intellectual development that he did?

Paul Baran's Concept of the Intellectual

Though we are not able to provide a precise psychological description of the developmental process by which he acquired the traits that were characteristic of his personality, one way of understanding E.A. Partridge is by viewing him in the context of Paul Baran's concept of the intellectual. The term "intellectual," as used here, is different from the way in which the term is typically used in everyday conversation. The usage of the term here is based on the work of Baran, who argues that intellectuals are people with special qualities and are distinguished not by the particular job they perform, but rather by the way they think, approach life, and understand the world.

Baran, in his book *The Longer View*, began his discussion of the social role of the intellectual with a simple question: "What is an intellectual?" His answer makes it clear that an intellectual is not necessarily "a person working with his intellect, relying for his livelihood ... on his brain rather than on his brawn" (p. 3). Indeed, Baran is quite explicit in arguing that a person's occupation itself has little to do with whether or not he or she is an intellectual. Baran argues that those who make a living by engaging in intellectual as opposed to physical labour are intellect workers. The intellect workers typically are "individuals working with their minds rather than with their muscles, living off their wits rather than off their hands" (p. 3). We must be very clear that intellect workers are not necessarily intellectuals, indeed most often they are not. ·

What, then, is an intellectual? Baran's answer is found in a definition which focusses not on occupation, but on the individual's interest in, and capacity to look at and understand, human society as a totality. Baran's intellectual has, as Mills put it, a certain "quality of mind." Baran argues that the intellectual may be an industrial worker, artisan, farmer or any other occupation:

> what marks the intellectual and distinguishes him from the intellect worker and indeed from all others is that his concern with the entire historical process is not a tangential interest but permeates his thought and significantly affects his work. ... it is this effort to interconnect which constitutes one of the intellectual's outstanding characteristics. (p. 8)

Baran went on to argue that the intellectual is vitally interested in "the dynamics and evolution of the social order itself" (p. 9). In addition, the intellectual is vitally motivated by, and committed to, the values of humanism and a humanitarian world view. Indeed, Baran (1969: 12) stated that this is essential to being an intellectual:

> This is the issue on which the intellectual cannot compromise. Disagreements, arguments, and bitter struggles are unavoidable and, indeed, indispensable to ascertain the nature, and the means to the realization, of conditions necessary for the health, development, and happiness of men. But the adherence to humanism, the insistence on the principle that the quest for human advancement requires no scientific or logical justification, constitutes what might be called the axiomatic foundation of all meaningful intellectual effort, an axiomatic foundation without the acceptance of which an individual can neither consider himself nor be thought of as an intellectual.

A final point warrants mention, the treatment often afforded intellectuals. Committed as they are to penetrating and radical analysis in their search for the truth, intellectuals can expect to be "decried as unscientific and speculative and ... punished by professional discrimination, social ostracism, and outright intimidation" (Baran, 1969: 13-14). This is because "An intellectual is ... in essence a *social critic*, a person whose concern is to identify, to analyze, and in this way to help to overcome the obstacles barring the way to the attainment of a better, more humane, and more rational social order" (Baran, 1969: 14).

A key capacity of Baran's intellectual is the ability to take "the longer view," to analyze the larger picture, and to be concerned with what we might term "the totality." The concept of totality is central to the kind of critical thinking which Partridge exemplified. The notion of grasping and understanding social reality as a totality demands that each aspect of that reality be understood in the context of all other aspects, and that the whole be understood as dynamic, constantly changing, developing and in process. The larger whole must be understood as the context in which we place and understand the parts. Partridge's analysis of poverty is a case in point, meaning that he knew that a social phenomenon like poverty could only be understood when placed in the context of the class relations and dynamics that determine the social distribution of wealth. Further, this conception of social reality implies that the various aspects of any given social structure be viewed not as a harmonious whole but one containing potential contradictions and conflicts.

E.A. Partridge as an Intellectual

The writings that Partridge left us contain numerous illustrations of how his thoughts and actions were those of an intellectual. By way of illustration, we might consider the central issue Partridge addressed in his book — poverty. Poverty and the plight of the poor, Partridge argued, must be systematically understood within the context of the class structures of capitalist society and the presence of the rich. Poverty and wealth were both generated by the class structure of capitalist society. In Partridge's words:

> To abolish poverty then would be to abolish class distinctions, — which cannot long survive comparative economic equality — and with the disappearance of these, *class rule* must disappear; and of necessity, government by a class, in the interest of that class, must be replaced by a government so expressive of the common will... . (pp. 32-33)

Perhaps the central intellectual capacity involved in the type of thinking and analysis which grasp reality as a totality is the ability to analytically penetrate the surface appearance of phenomena. Partridge's works are replete with examples of how he understood that things are not really as they seem to be. Partridge argued, for example, that the great patriotic cause that those who died in Word War I were fighting for "turned out to be in essence a sordid squabble among traders, merchants, using the term in its wider sense, those seeking trade, these defending what they had" (p. 74). Partridge further demonstrated this mode of analytical thinking within the context of his discussion of the origins of profits. In comments clearly designed to counter the conventional view that profits simply accrue as a reward to those who risk capital, Partridge argued that profits must be understood as part of the exploitive social relations of capitalist society:

> Capitalism stands for monopoly of ownership in the means of production, distribution, and exchange of wealth, and consequent mastership, involving exploitation, of those who do not own. Capitalists, when not too drunken with power and the pride of possession, know that despite their *legal* title, they have no *moral* right to monopolize the *natural resources of a people, either by purchase or lease,* or other methods of securing them; they know also that as for the *artificial means for supplying the people's needs,* the disinherited ones who operate them as hired servants, have in the mass, paid for them over and over again by the excess of their earnings over what they received in pay since starting to work for wages. (p. 47)

Associated with this mode of thinking and analyzing the world is the related assumption that nothing, as it exists, is "the final product." Put somewhat differently, Partridge viewed the universe as a dynamic process, always changing and developing. This is apparent in his comment of the world as being "presumably only half-finished" (p. 7), and his many remarks on the unrealized potential that exists in "human nature." Perhaps the point is best illustrated in the following remarks which follow a discussion of the more negative features of capitalist society:

But the cloud is not without its silver lining. Signs multiply to show that this malignant, individualistic, catch-as-catch-can, dog-eat-dog scheme of things, wherein it is counted not a matter of shame, but rather of pride, to be a parasite, is nearing its end. Mortification has set in; and it is comforting to reflect it is the way of Nature that out of death and decay she brings new and shining forms of life. In this lies the hope that within the old festering, disintegrating, social organism, the elements of a wholesome, desirable community life are even now coming into being. (p. 85)

An associated but not identical characteristic of the Baran's intellectual is a persistent interest in the dynamics and evolution of the social order. If there is a dominant theme in Partridge's thinking it is found in his persistent efforts to understand the nature of the social changes that were occurring around him. He clearly understood that his society was a dynamic one, changing and evolving before his eyes:

"Whatever is, is best" in our socio-economic order, even when "best administered," only till we can evolve something that better fits our need. There is nothing sacred or settled about our present social, economic, and political institutions any more than about those that preceded them; they are merely the latest experiments, — mostly highly unsuccessful — that "mankind in the making" has made; "the things that are" hastening to make way for "the things that shall be." (p. 20)

He succinctly summarized this point in the following manner: "No institution is eternal; no institution can stay with us inevitably" (p. 20).

A final illustration of Partridge's interest in the larger dynamics of Canadian social and economic development involves his views on the historical role of the West in Canadian industrialization:

The history of Canada since Confederation — the outcome of the politico-commercial, or a Commercio-political conspiracy, if consequences are any indication of motives — has been a history of heartless robbery of both the people of the Maritimes and of the Prairie Sections of Canada by the Big "Vested" Interests — so called from the size of their owners' vests — of the politically and financially stronger Central Provinces. ... In the case of the Prairie Provinces there has been the most bare-faced robbery of their provincial rights in the matter of their lands, including resources of timber, minerals, fishing waters and sources of natural power. (pp. 77-78)

Beneath the outrage which Partridge's rhetoric displays there was a deeply held humanistic value system. Indeed, Partridge's entire life was guided by his humanism. The depth of his commitment to the improvement of his fellow human beings has been alluded to earlier, and here we need only to reinforce the point with the final words of his book:

Let us agree to forego the spending of our means on luxuries while any are without the necessities and decencies of life. Let us make men, women, and children, not money, people, not property, the center of our interest. ... Society must develop such solidarity that the care of each must be the concern of all. Men must not be forced to pay for the protection of the law for person or property; to perish for need of a physician through lack of a fee; to mortgage their future for the burial of their dead; to see their children grow up without preparation for the business of life, without culture or calling, because of lack of opportunity, for any cause whatever. (p. 224)

The final aspect of Baran's portrait of an intellectual that is appropriate when considering the life of E.A. Partridge relates to the treatment accorded the intellectual within the larger society. Baran's claim (1969: 12) that "Disagreements, arguments, and bitter struggles are unavoidable" holds true in the case of Partridge. Partridge faced opposition to his various proposals and views, opposition which never left him pessimistic or ready to give up. Many individuals would have shrunk from the treatment accorded him by members of the grain trade on the occasion of his first investigative visit to Winnipeg in 1903. Many would have abandoned the idea of a producer-controlled cooperative after the reception he received within the TGGA on his return. In *A War on Poverty* Partridge frequently acknowledged the fact that his ideas and arguments might appear too radical. He opened the book with a statement that indicated he was prepared to face his critics openly:

Surely it is no sign of a fool or a fanatic to decry our present methods in the light of the manner in which multitudes are forced to live under them; nor an evidence of moral depravity to suggest alternative ones for trial! (p. vi)

Elsewhere he declared: "We suffer not from visionaries, but from those who lack vision. It can not be too often repeated: 'Where there is no vision the people perish'" (p. 13).

As we saw, Baran noted that the intellectual is not necessarily the most popular or well-liked person in the community, indeed that person is often met with hostility. Hostile reactions to Partridge's varied proposals were common, as witnessed by the 1910 meeting of the SGGA. It is clear that resistance to Partridge's ideas arose out of the class position of the agricultural producer. The agrarian *petite bourgeoisie*, as a class, was clearly in a subservient position, economically, socially and politically, to key sections of the dominant class. However, the farmers were also a part of the property system that comprised a capitalist society with some vested interest in the property relations of that society. To expect such a class to support, *en masse*, radical propositions for the elimination of

84

private property would not be realistic, particularly at a time when the agrarian class was expanding and to some degree prospering.

Partridge, then, was part of a mass-based class protest against certain specific aspects of the Canadian social structure. He was part of a series of limited transformations of that social structure through cooperative and collective efforts. He was part of the emergence of agrarian-based associations, economic cooperatives and political parties. He was part of an historic transformation of an entire region through settlement and then what might be called "unsettlement."

While it is clear that many of Partridge's associates and contemporaries understood the problems they faced in largely regional terms, and while it is also clear that Partridge shared in this level of analysis, his analysis went deeper. It is appropriate to understand the agrarian movement in which Partridge played such a key role as a class-based phenomenon. The West and its agrarian population emerged at a specific historical moment because of the needs of industrial and commercial capital based in central Canada. The agrarian *petite bourgeoisie* of western Canada was thus a part of a larger strategy of capital accumulation.

It was his understanding of the nature of the relations between classes in capitalist society that served to give his analysis its radical edge. It was through the prism of class analysis that Partridge came to understand the limitations of the various reforms that he had been a part of over the years. In the final analysis he came to argue that these reforms did not alter the fundamental relations of exploitation and domination that characterize production and accumulation in a capitalist society.

Final Comment: Biography and History

Partridge must be understood, like all human beings, within the context of the society in which he lived. Humans are unique in a number of ways, not the least of which is the fact that we are both products and producers of our social structures. Each of us has a unique individual history, a biography, that tells the story of the many factors and influences that helped to make us what we are. Embedded in our biographies are the records of our family, educational, work, religious, political and a host of other experiences. These biographies are very much alive, changing and developing as new experiences impact on us.

As C.W. Mills notes, human beings, with their unique biographies, are inseparable from the historical period in which they move. As humans, we are pushed, pulled, moulded and transformed by the social structures and historical forces within which we live. However, what is truly unique about the human condition is the fact that the very structures and historical processes that have such a vital impact on us are themselves the outcome and the product of human actions. Humans must be understood not only as products but also as producers, moulders, creators and makers of the very social structures which have such a profound impact on them. It is in this way that biography and history intersect, and it is in this way that we must understand the remarkable history of E.A. Partridge.

As we have seen, Partridge was part of a remarkable historical process through which Canada was transformed into an industrial capitalist society, in part through a series of deliberate state actions. We know that the settlement of the West was an integral part of an industrialization process from Confederation to the Depression of the 1930s. We also know that this process involved the deliberate establishment of a population of agrarian producers who were to serve as a domestic market protected by the tariffs established in 1879. The conflicts that emerged in the West were a direct outcome of the role of the agrarian producers in the development strategy undertaken by the federal government and supported by central Canadian industry. To put the matter very simply, there was a western Canadian agrarian movement because agricultural producers came to understand the nature of the economic and political processes underway. Partridge played a central role in that process because his characteristics as an intellectual seemed to crystallize his thinking. Partridge was able to grasp the nature of the relations of power which were unfolding in Canada. He came to understand the historic importance of the relations of wealth creation and appropriation that were emerging as industrial development occurred. He came to understand the relationship between economic and political power and he increasingly articulated this understanding in critical social analysis.

It is clear then that it was the operation of the Canadian economic and political system — the actions of the grain trade, the impact of the tariff, the concentration of wealth and power and the structures of political power — that came to radicalize Partridge. Partridge and his partners in the agrarian movement, in turn, had an impact on the social, economic and political structures. However, Partridge became increasingly convinced that these changes were not significant and radical enough. The involvement of farmers in the grain trade through their own grain companies did not alter the basic inequalities that the operation of the capitalist markets produced. The involvement of farmers in party politics did not alter the fact that political power seemed to be structurally tied to the great centres of economic power that market society produced. The distinction between political power and the holding of political power became apparent to Partridge.

In examining Partridge's critical social analysis, it is essential to consider his abiding humanism. My final comments will dwell on this.

It is impossible when reflecting on Partridge's life at a personal level not to marvel at the fact that he retained an optimism and love of life even after the string of personal tragedies that he and Mary endured. The loss of his leg and the subsequent pain and misery would have destroyed many people. For Partridge, it was merely an inconvenience. The loss of three children in a space of four years, events whose impact defies analysis, was borne by Partridge and his wife without shrinking into self-pity or bitter resentments. How? Although it must remain speculation, the unending faith in both a Creator and its product — humanity — seems to have been essential. Partridge had a mission, a goal, an objective in life which went beyond even his immediate family. The betterment of humankind was his goal — what mortal hindrances could deter him from this objective?

During the year he was working on *A War on Poverty* a young man from Manitoba, Normal Turnbull, spent the winter at the Partridge home, partly acting as a secretary for Partridge. Among the lasting impressions made on Turnbull was Partridge's passion for justice, love of life, and sense of humour. His was an undaunted spirit that demanded to know and to understand, and which required expression.

The understanding and knowledge which Partridge sought out and acted upon was often of a different variety than was common in his society. Partridge's capacity and his desire for visionary thinking was made possible by his mode of thought. What we mean by his mode of thought is the capacity to see beyond the present and to envision and anticipate possibilities and potentials. What distinguishes the visionary and the utopian is their capacity to consider possibilities beyond the present. To remain forever locked in the present is to sentence humanity to only what it has. To foresee potentials and to work for their realization makes possible the sorts of advances, transformations and developments that characterize human history. What was unique about Partridge was his capacity to apply this mode of thought on a continual and systematic basis. The mode of thought that Partridge epitomized saw any and all reality as transient, as passing, as in a real sense "unreal," because it contains possibilities and potentials which, when realized, will transfer that reality.

Perhaps there are no more fitting final words from Partridge than one of his last written communications. Partridge closed a letter sent to be read at the 1931 meeting of UFC, Saskatchewan Section with the following remarks:

> There is nothing sinister nor immoral in the radical proposals outlined above, however revolutionary they may appear to those who are unaccustomed to trace social and economic conditions back to their root causes. They are merely evolutionary changes in law, in

custom, and in behaviour that must take place before Isaiah's prophecy is fulfilled among us, and it can be truthfully affirmed of our common people, and they shall build houses and inhabit them; they shall plant vineyards; and eat the fruit of them. They shall not build and another inhabit; they shall not plant and another eat.

Bibliography

Archer, John. 1980. *Saskatchewan: A History*. Saskatoon: Western Producer Prairie Books.

Baran, Paul. 1969. *The Longer View*. New York: Monthly Review Press.

Bliss, J.M. (ed.). 1966. *Canadian History in Documents, 1763-1966*. Toronto: Ryerson.

Bocking, D.H. 1979. *Pages from the Past: Essays on Saskatchewan History*. Saskatoon: Western Producer Prairie Books.

Boyd, Hugh. 1938. *New Breaking: An Outline of Co-operation Among the Western Farmers of Canada*. Toronto: J.M. Dent and Sons.

Brown, Lorne. 1969. "The Progressive Tradition in Saskatchewan," *Our Generation* 6 (4):21-46.

Canada. House of Commons. 1880, 1899. *Debates*.

Careless, J.M.S. 1963. *Canada: A Story of Challenge*. Toronto: Macmillan.

Chodos, Robert. 1973. *The CPR: A Century of Corporate Welfare*. Toronto: James Lormier and Company.

Clarke, S.D. 1939. *The Canadian Manufacturers' Association*. Toronto: University of Toronto Press.

Colquette, R. 1957. *The First Fifty Years: A History of United Grain Growers Limited*. Winnipeg: The Public Press.

Conway, John. 1984. *The West: The History of a Region in Confederation*. Toronto: James Lorimer and Company.

Davis, A.K. 1971. "Canadian Society as Hinterland Versus Metropolis." In *Canadian Society: Pluralism, Conflict and Change*, edited by R. Ossenberg. Scarborough: Prentice Hall.

Davisson, Walter. 1927. *Pooling Wheat In Canada*. Ottawa: Graphic Publishers.

Fairbairn, Garry. 1984. *From Prairie Roots*. Saskatoon: Western Producer Prairie Books.

Fowke, Vernon. 1947. *Canadian Agricultural Policy: The Historical Pattern*. Toronto: University of Toronto Press.

——. 1957. *The National Policy and the Wheat Economy*. Toronto: University of Toronto Press.

Gallagher, John. 1983. *To Kill The Crow*. Moose Jaw: Challenge Publishers.

Grain Growers Record, 1906 to 1943. 1944. Winnipeg: United Grain Growers Limited.

Hedlin, R. 1960. "Edmund [*sic*] A. Partridge." *Papers of the Historical and Scientific Society of Manitoba* 3 (15).

Innis, H.A. 1962. *Essays in Canadian Economic History*. Toronto: University of Toronto Press.

Knuttila, K. Murray. 1975. "The Saskatchewan Agrarian Movement 1900-1930: A Case Study of Populism." M.A. thesis, University of Regina.

Laycock, David. 1990. *Populism and Democratic Thought in the Canadian Prairies, 1910 to 1945.* Toronto: University of Toronto Press.

Lipset, S.M. 1971. *Agrarian Socialism: The Cooperative Commonwealth Federation in Saskatchewan.* Berkeley: University of California Press.

Lower, A.R.M. 1964. *Colony to Nation.* Don Mills: Longmans Canada Limited.

MacGibbon, D.A. 1952. *The Canadian Grain Trade 1931-1951.* Toronto: University of Toronto Press.

Mackintosh. W.A. 1924. *Agricultural Cooperation in Western Canada.* Kingston: Queen's University Press.

——. 1935. *The Economic Problems of the Prairie Provinces.* Toronto: Macmillan.

——. 1939. *The Economic Background of Dominion-Provincial Relations.* Ottawa: King's Printer.

MacKirdy, K.A., J.S. Moir, and Y.F. Zoltvany. 1971. *Changing Perspectives in Canadian History: Selected Problems.* Don Mills: J.M. Dent and Sons.

Macpherson, C.B. 1953. *Democracy in Alberta: Social Credit and the Party System.* Toronto: University of Toronto Press.

Martin, Chester. 1973. *Dominion Lands Policy.* Toronto: McClelland and Stewart.

McCrorie, James N. 1964. *In Union is Strength.* Saskatoon: Centre for Community Studies.

—— 1971. "Change and Paradox in Agrarian Social Movements." In *Canadian Society: Pluralism, Conflict and Change,* edited by R. Ossenberg. Scarborough: Prentice Hall.

Mills, C.W. 1959. *The Sociological Imagination.* New York: Oxford University Press.

Moorhouse, H. 1918. *Deep Furrows.* Toronto: George McLeod Limited.

Morton, A.S. 1938. *History of Prairie Settlement.* Toronto: Macmillian.

Morton, W.L. 1950. *The Progressive Party in Canada.* Toronto: University of Toronto Press.

Myers, Gustavus. [1914] 1972. *A History of Canadian Wealth.* Toronto: James Lewis and Samuel Publications.

Naylor, R.T. 1975. *The History of Canadian Business.* 2 vols. Toronto: James Lorimer and Company.

Nesbitt, Leonard. n.d. *Tides in the West.* Saskatoon: Modern Press.

Palmer, Howard (ed.). 1977. *The Settlement of the West.* Calgary: Comprint Publishing, University of Calgary.

Partridge, E.A. 1925. *A War on Poverty: The One War That Can End War.* Winnipeg: Wallingford Press.

Patton, Harold. 1928. *Grain Growers' Cooperation in Western Canada.* Cambridge: Harvard University Press.

Pentland, H. Clare. 1981. *Labour and Capital in Canada 1650-1860.* Toronto: James Lorimer and Company.

90

Ryerson, Stanley. 1968. *Unequal Union: Roots of Conflict in the Canadas, 1815-1873.* Toronto: Progress Books.

Stanley, George. 1964. *The Birth of Western Canada: A History of the Riel Rebellions.* Toronto: Ryerson Press.

Waite, P.B. (ed.). 1963. *The Confederation Debates in the Province of Canada, 1865.* Toronto: McClelland and Stewart.

Wilson, C.F. 1978. *A Century of Canadian Grain: Government Policy to 1951.* Saskatoon: Western Producer Prairie Books.

——. 1979. *Canadian Grain Marketing.* Winnipeg: Canadian International Grains Institute.

Wood, L.A. 1924. *A History of Farmers' Movements in Canada.* Toronto: Ryerson.

Wright, J.F.C.1955. *Saskatchewan: The History of a Province.* Toronto: McClelland and Stewart.

——. 1956. *Prairie Progress: Consumer Co-operation in Saskatchewan.* Saskatoon: Modern Press.

Yates, S.W. 1947. *The Saskatchewan Wheat Pool: Its Origin, Organization and Progress, 1924-1935.* Saskatoon: United Farmers of Canada.

Young, Walter. 1969. *The Anatomy of a Party: The National CCF, 1932-61.* Toronto: University of Toronto Press.

Zakuta, L.A. 1964. *A Protest Movement Becalmed: A Study of Change in the CCF.* Toronto: University of Toronto Press.

ARCHIVE SOURCES

Saskatchewan Archives Board-Regina

Biography - Partridge E.A.

Clippings File: Farm Movement E 1

Clippings File: Farmers Political Association

Clippings File: Sintaluta

Grain Elevators / Trade File

Herperger, Joseph H. 1968. "Edward Alexander Partridge and W.C. Paynter." Unpublished paper for History N 435, University of Regina.

Partridge Family History R - E 531

Partridge Papers A 118

Pamphlet File : Grain

Pamphlet File : SGGA

Pamphlet File: Agricultural societies

Pamphlet File: Canadian Council of Agriculture

Pamphlet File: Co-operative societies

Pamphlet File: Farmers Union of Canada

Pamphlet File: Saskatchewan Farmers Union

Railton, Anne (Partridge) II. A. 118

Saskatchewan Grain Growers' Association annual convention records

Territorial Grain Growers' Association annual convention records

UFC (SS) Holdings B2 - VII.1

UGG Limited

National Archives of Canada

The Home Bank of Canada Records, MG 28, II 11

United Grain Growers Archives, Winnipeg

E.A. Partridge 1861-1931 File

Queen's University Archives

Crerar Papers (Partridge letters), Coll. 2117, Series III

NEWSPAPERS AND PERIODICALS

Regina Standard

Saskatchewan Co-operative Elevator Company Ltd. News

Grain Growers' Guide

The Voice

The Western Producer

Winnipeg Free Press

E.A. PARTRIDGE

"Mr. Partridge's Address," 10th Annual Convention SGGA

"A Farmers Trade Union." 1907. Pamphlet, United Grain Growers Archives.

"Shall We Co-operate to Secure Legitimate Value for Our Wheat." 1905. Pamphlet, United Grain Growers Archives.

"The Proposes People's Hudson's Bay Railway Company." n.d. Pamphlet, United Grain Growers Archives.

"A People's Road to Hudson's Bay" n.d. Pamphlet United Grain Growers Archives.

Messages delivered to Annual General Meeting United Farmers of Canada (Saskatchewan Section), 1930 and 1931. Saskatchewan Archives Board.

"Government Ownership and Control of Elevators," 7th Annual Convention SGGA.

"Report of Ottawa Delegation," 8th Annual Convention SGGA.

"How May the Grain Growers' Association be Made More Useful and Permanent," 4th Annual Convention TGGA.

Address to 6th Annual Convention SGGA.

"Mr. Partridge's Letter" - read to 9th Annual Convention SGGA.

"Report on Trip," 5th Annual Convention TGGA.

Index

DATE DUE

"That Man Partridge"